The Cheap Diva's Guide to Frugal and Fabulous Living

How to Shop Smart, Look Your Best, Decorate with Style, and Have Fun for Less Money!

ISBN 978-0-9825296-0-7

Printed in the United States of America.

Booklocker.com, Inc.
2010

The Cheap Diva's Guide to Frugal and Fabulous Living

How to Shop Smart, Look Your Best, Decorate with Style, and Have Fun for Less Money!

By

Stephanie Ann

Dedication

I must thank my wonderful family for believing in me and encouraging me to pursue my dreams. Their love and support means more to me than words can say.

I would also like to thank everyone who supported me by cheering me on with their kind words or by simply reading thecheapdiva.com blog and reminding me that I am not alone in my quest to be frugal and fabulous.

Table of Contents

Introduction

With so many books on budget living the obvious question is, what makes me an expert on living well for less? For starters, I was living the frugal lifestyle long before it was fashionable. For many years I have chosen to drive a used car in good condition, live in affordable one-bedroom apartments instead of spending more money on more spacious digs, shop at Target and Wal-Mart for cheap clothes, take advantage of clearance sales at better department stores for nicer clothes, and avoid expensive purchases that would lead to debt, unless they were absolutely necessary. A "necessary" purchase would be buying another used car when the old one inconveniently dies on the freeway, only to restart, die, restart, and then cruise into the nearest town at a painfully slow pace. Yes, that really did happen to me. (I would personally like to thank whoever invented the cell phone, because it allowed me to get assistance in a slightly less hysterical manner than if I hadn't had a phone.)

I would love to claim that all of this frugal living was part of some great long-term plan to save up to start a business or build my dream house, but that's not how it happened. My frugal lifestyle is a result of getting stuck in a series of low-paying jobs that were routinely interrupted by periods of unemployment. Over the years this pattern of being employed long enough to catch up on bills and save some money, only to use up a good chunk of my savings when the job ended, made me develop a healthy sense of mistrust for employers. This lack of trust lead to healthy savings habits that served me well when a boss delivered the inevitable "You're doing a great job, but unfortunately the job you are doing so well has been eliminated" speech. I have seen other, more naïve employees turn their cubicles into personal shrines full of photos and nostalgic memorabilia. I, on the other hand, have demonstrated an impressive, businesslike efficiency by bringing nothing but my purse, my lunch, and myself to work. This has allowed me to clean out my cubicle and leave that dead-end job behind faster than you can say "filing for unemployment."

For years I had a negative attitude about living cheaply. I thought of frugal living as something to be tolerated until I earned the type of income that would allow me to buy nice things, eat at fine restaurants regularly, and spend more freely without worrying about draining my savings account. At some point I finally decided I was not going to put the good life on hold waiting for decent-paying job. I started focusing on enjoying myself more and expressing my sense of style in ways that wouldn't break the bank. This shift in attitude--from being preoccupied with financial survival to focusing on living well for less--was empowering. Once I started looking at my options instead of looking longingly at the stuff I couldn't afford, a world of possibilities opened up. I realized that being fabulous has more to do with the right attitude than anything else.

My favorite story about being frugal while having a fabulous attitude comes from an article I read in the local paper. A group of women definitely past prom age liked to get dressed up in old prom dresses for a special day out. On this special day out, one of their husbands acted as a designated driver while the women sat in the back of the minivan sipping champagne and listening to their favorite oldies tunes, happily singing along whenever the mood struck.

These women spent their special day in fancy dresses, laughing with one another and being chauffeured around to local shopping destinations. So, what were the fabulous shopping destinations that they got all dressed up for? Garage sales! Not fancy estate sales, mind you, but typical all-American garage sales full of outdated electronics and unfashionable clothes. They took a nonevent like garage-sale shopping and turned it into a marvelous and memorable occasion. As Jean Webster once said, "It isn't the great big pleasures that count the most; it's making a great deal out of the little ones."

The Secret to Frugal and Fabulous Living

I have discovered that mastering the art of frugal and fabulous living has more to do with making the most of what you have than with the size of your bank account. To truly live well you need to focus on opportunities for experiencing the finer things in life now instead of simply settling for less until your finances improve.

The first thing to let go of is the "all or nothing" mentality. It's easy to look at some millionaire's home on a TV show and think "I'll never be able to live in a home like that!" Just because you might not be able to experience the lifestyle of the rich and famous every day doesn't mean you can't experience it at all. There are historic mansions that have been turned into bed and breakfast businesses, and luxury hotels with spa amenities that would be happy to treat you like a VIP. A weekend spent in fabulous luxury is certainly better than a lifetime spent whining about what you can't have.

A little planning can go a long way toward getting what you want. For years my family paid for vacations partially through selling stuff through a local consignment store. The money from the things we sold went into a bank account that was used strictly for family vacations. When the travel account wasn't full enough for an expensive vacation, we simply visited local attractions, museums, botanical gardens, and so forth, acting like tourists without the expense of distant travel. When the travel account reached a certain point, we chose a destination and sought out the best travel deals. By the time we got around to taking a trip, one family member had accumulated enough frequent-flier miles on her credit card to help cover the cost of plane tickets, which greatly reduced travel expenses.

You might have the money to treat yourself to something special without realizing it. I used to buy a $2 celebrity lifestyle magazine every Friday to read during my lunch break to take my mind off of my painfully boring job. After weeks of buying it, I did the math and realized that this magazine, which I threw in the trash after one reading, would end up costing me $100 a year! For $100 I could get a nice facial from an upscale salon. Even if I only got one facial a year, the pampering benefits of the facial far outweighed some mediocre magazine whose entertainment value was easily replaced by watching the TV in the employee break room. The more you say "no" to small expenses for things that add little value to your life, the more money you will have for the finer things.

A resourceful bargain hunter knows that just because something is normally expensive doesn't mean it's always going to be expensive. Sometimes high-ticket items can be had for free or very little. Popular contests provide an opportunity to win free trips, new cars, and even free homes! It's possible to attend expensive charity galas or theatrical performances for free simply by volunteering for those organizations. Once-expensive merchandise can end up drastically cut in price due to going-out-of-business sales, being last year's model, or being property seized by police and sold to the public. Learning to keep your eyes open for opportunities that bring the things you want within reach allows you to live large even on a small budget.

Part One: Money

"Too many people spend money they haven't earned, to buy things they don't want, to impress people they don't like."

--Will Rogers

Easy Ways to Make Extra Money

Getting the Most Cash for Your Clutter

Before you break out the garage sale signs, consider other selling strategies that require less time and effort yet generate a bigger payoff than the average garage sale. A garage sale is a time-consuming way to unload unwanted items. Hours are spent organizing and pricing merchandise just to have the customers who do show up try to haggle over prices that were dirt cheap to begin with. After it's finally over, unsold leftovers must be put away until they can be disposed of somehow (a bonfire in your driveway perhaps?). Clearly, this is not the most rewarding way to spend a weekend.

Some things are better suited to an online outlet, like eBay, than a consignment store. Certain kinds of vintage clothing and collectibles will bring higher prices at auction than at consignment as a result of competitive bidding. Ideally, you will attract at least two competitive-bordering-on-crazy, money-is-no-object bidders who drive the price of your knickknacks way up. Compare items you want to sell to similar items on eBay. Is anyone bidding on the items? What prices are they going for?

Providing prospective buyers with lots of information helps ease any doubts they have about buying from you. When shopping on eBay or another online outlet, people need to feel comfortable about their purchase, or they won't buy. Entice prospective buyers by giving a detailed description of the item and taking a picture of it from different sides. Fuzzy, poorly lit photographs and vague descriptions may cause the buyer to either request better photos and more information, or simply ignore the item altogether. Amazon.com is great for selling books and other media. One of the benefits of selling through Amazon is that your item is linked to the regular-priced item being sold there. A customer looking up an item sees next to Amazon's regular retail price a link to a list of independent sellers like you. This allows savvy customers to instantly compare prices and see who is offering the best deals.

You may think your CD from a one-hit-wonder band is a classic collectible, but does the band have a cult following that could earn you some serious cash? Or are its current CD prices so cheap the CD is more useful as a drink coaster than a moneymaker? To see whether it's worth the time to try to sell your DVD or CD online, look up your item on eBay. By clicking on the Completed listings button on the left-hand side of the eBay page, you can see what people are willing to pay for that item.

Stores specializing in used DVDs and CDs will buy your discs for a lot less than you probably paid for them. Stores selling used media are an option if you have a lot of discs that aren't worth much and you don't want to take the time to sell them online.

Last and in many ways least, there are used book stores. They will happily buy your books for far less than their original retail price, so try not to have a heart attack when they offer you $1.78 for your complete set of mint-condition hardback books. Used book stores are good for selling stuff that isn't worth your time to try to sell through other methods. Old magazines that aren't old enough to be considered vintage and paperback books so cheap the cost of shipping to a customer is more expensive than the book itself are good candidates for a used book store. They sometimes buy CDs and DVDs as well as books.

An alternative to trying to sell your stuff is to donate it. Talk to your accountant about the tax advantages of donating. IRS Publication 561, "Determining the Value of Donated Property" (http://www.irs.gov/), provides guidelines for putting an accurate dollar amount on your donations. No matter what the value of your donation, be sure to get a receipt for your tax records.

For me, getting rid of stuff is a liberating process that allows me to focus on the things that enhance my lifestyle without the distraction of unwanted clutter. It also allows me the handy cash I need to go out and buy more stuff! (Just kidding…sort of.)

Words That Work

Using the right words is key to selling your stuff faster and for more money. Keywords are specific terms most likely to pique the interest of potential buyers. They can be the brand, the model, the year the item was made, the materials it is made of, the name of an artist related to the item, and so forth. I collect vintage cameras because I believe displaying a collection is more personal and interesting than home decor that looks as if you hit the shopping mall intent on finding a picture to match your sofa. One of the best deals I got on eBay was on a rare vintage underwater camera from a seller who didn't use any keywords. Other sellers who mentioned the brand, model, or even the fact that it was an underwater camera in their descriptions sold that exact same model for much more money.

To identify the words most likely to attract attention from potential buyers, do an Internet search for the item you are selling and see what words people use to sell items similar to yours. The features or benefits mentioned by different sellers repeatedly are the ones buyers are looking for. Include this information in your sales pitch. This approach works for selling items on eBay, through a classified ad, or just about any other sales channel.

Words describing the condition of the item can be a useful selling tool. The phrase “mint condition” is music to the ears of prospective buyers. But when I see the phrase “in good condition for its age” my first thought is “So am I! Now tell me something useful!” Whether the object being sold is gently used or it looks as if it was run over by a bus, choose words that give an accurate description of the condition of the item and identify any flaws. When it comes to selling, it pays to be accurate and honest with your buyers.

Cashing in on Consignment Stores

I remember my first attempt at selling some clothes at a local consignment store. I selected several classic pieces appropriate for a conservative office environment and in excellent condition. When I set down the clothing in front of her, the store owner looked at me as though I had just dumped a dead squirrel on her counter. In a tone that made no effort to hide her disgust, she told me the store preferred to sell designer brands only. This was news to me, since the merchandise I saw around me wasn’t exactly dazzling me with its stylishness or designer influence. I walked out with $12 for my stuff and a valuable lesson: Do your homework before hitting the consignment stores.

Different consignment stores appeal to different types of customers. Is the consignment store you want to work with a trendy clothing store aimed at the junior-size market? A plus-size store? A higher-end designer consignment store? To determine which consignment store would be the best match for your unwanted clothing, call before making a trip.

Consignment stores often have specific requirements for the types of clothing they take. Some stores only accept certain brands in clean and excellent condition that were bought within the last few years. Consignment stores may refuse to sell certain items, so ask about any off-limits merchandise before you bring your stuff in.

Timing plays an important part in selling clothes on consignment. Consignment stores have specific buying schedules. Don't try to sell a winter coat at the beginning of the summer, for example. Consignment stores also have specific times when they are willing to accept items for consignment. Don't just drop by, expecting them to be delighted by the prospect of looking at your piles of unwanted clothing in the middle of a busy Saturday. Call ahead.

When selling your stuff, ask about the markdown policy. Does the store automatically mark down merchandise after a certain point, or do you have the option of not having your clothes marked down? Some consignment stores will give you the option of paying you on the spot for your stuff, while other stores only pay you a portion of the sale price after the items sell.

The contract you get from a consignment store should document the payment schedule, mention any fees, and address the issue of lost or stolen items. When selling something of great value, like vintage jewelry, be sure the consignment store has fire and theft insurance. Get a receipt that lists every item you offer through the consignment store, and keep a photocopy of it in a separate location from the original receipt. The receipt should briefly identify prices as well as items. You don't want to discover the store owner priced your like-new cashmere sweater for $1.50 after the item has sold and there is nothing you can do about it. Once you get past the fact that you will end up selling your clothes for a lot less than you originally paid for them, you can start to enjoy less-cluttered closets and more cash.

Unloading Unwanted Furniture

Whether you are upgrading from the cheap off-the-shelf "some assembly required" furniture to "real" furniture, or just getting rid of something that no longer fits your taste and lifestyle, it's tempting to just dump it at the curb and let a random passerby pick it up. That may be the easiest way to get rid of furniture, but it's not the most profitable.

For virtually disposable particle-board student-dorm-quality furniture that has seen better days, consider including your unwanted furniture in a neighborhood garage sale, one where neighbors gather their stuff together and sell everything at one person's home instead of having separate garage sales. Or you may get a tax deduction by donating it to a thrift store. In general, the less the piece is worth, the less effort you should put into getting rid of it.

In general, eBay is one of the worst places to sell furniture, because of the high shipping costs involved. Unless you are selling a highly collectible piece of furniture where the shipping cost is of little concern to the buyer, skip eBay altogether and try other options.

For good quality furniture in good condition, say a solid-wood dresser, try local listings on craigslist.com. Post clear, sharp pictures of the piece from a couple of angles on your craigslist.com ad. Alongside the pictures state your asking price and the type of payment you accept (cash is best). Set up a free Google e-mail address that is separate from your personal e-mail address, and use it strictly for craigslist.com e-mails from potential buyers. This allows you to communicate with potential buyers without giving out personal information.

You can communicate with the buyer through e-mail to arrange a pick-up time and location for the item. Don't include your address or phone number in your ad. The only person who needs to know your home address and phone number is the person who commits to buying the furniture. Maybe you don't think your old couch is worth stealing, but a thief with low decorating standards might think otherwise. If the piece of furniture is so cumbersome that the buyer has to come to your home to pick it up, have a friend or relative on hand when the buyer comes by, just for safety's sake.

Where you sell depends on the quality of the furniture and how fast you want to get rid of it. For better quality furniture, try a furniture consignment store that sells high-quality furniture. This type of store attracts customers willing to spend the kind of money your furniture is worth, but it may take awhile to sell. For cheap furniture that would probably attract more dust than customers at a consignment store, college bulletin boards may be the better selling tool. The best months to sell your unwanted furniture are May and August, since those are popular times for moving.

Making Money from Magazines

If your busy life has made you an expert on figuring out how to do everyday tasks faster, cheaper, or more effectively, it's time to cash in on your ingenuity. Magazines--especially popular women's magazines--will sometimes pay for your helpful hints and problem-solving ideas.

To find magazines that pay good money for good ideas, visit a local library or retail store with a large magazine selection. Start browsing through magazines for their tips page. Take note of the guidelines for sending tips in, how much the publication pays for each tip, and the magazine's e-mail address for sending the tips.

When you get home, write down your best tips in brief paragraphs. Pick what you feel are you strongest tips, then send in the top five tips to the magazine that pays the most. Send another set of tips to another magazine on your list, and repeat this process for three to five magazines. Keep track of which tips got sent to which magazines. If one magazine doesn't use your tips, send them to other magazines until you either run out of magazines or run out of tips.

Having a talent for creating original dishes that your family and friends devour as though they are partaking in a pie-eating contest can be a recipe for success. A variety of magazines pay good money for original unpublished recipes. Some magazines have monthly recipe contests. Read the guidelines carefully, and look at the winning recipes in the magazine to get a taste of what the editors are looking for.

While magazines are a great way to earn a little extra cash, don't expect it to be fast cash. Magazines often take several weeks to publish and pay for the tips and recipes they feature. But when you start receiving checks in the mail they will come as a pleasant reminder that it really does pay to be resourceful.

Is a Direct Sales Business Right for You?

From Mary Kay to Tupperware, there is a direct sales company to suit every interest. Usually they try to recruit new sales representatives with the seductive promise that the product line is so fabulous it practically sells itself. The products may do many things, but selling themselves isn't one of them.

Successful direct sales representatives must be friendly, knowledgeable, and genuinely enthusiastic about the products they sell. They keep up to date on new sales promotions or products, and regularly generate sales by meeting new people, hosting home parties, maintaining contact with current customers, and recruiting other people to become sales reps for that product.

Direct sales companies not only supply you with products and promotional materials, but they also supply you with an established system for selling those products. They are not looking for creative thinkers; they are looking for people who will follow their system to the letter. Using their prestige cosmetics to paint cartoon characters on children's faces at the local craft show, for example, might not be their idea of appropriate marketing.

Before signing up with any direct sales company, ask the company representative some tough questions so you can be confident that you are investing both your time and money wisely. For starters, how much does it cost to begin in the business? Does the company pay for promotional materials like postcards and catalogs after you become a sales rep? Are you required to buy certain quantities of product or promotional materials to maintain your status as a sales rep? Is there a monthly quota of sales?

Be sure to ask how many people selling the same line of products are already in your area. You don't want to be inviting customers who are already loyal to another sales rep to your home parties. If home parties aren't convenient, then what are your other options for marketing? Could you sell merchandise through online sites such as eBay or at craft shows? If you decide to quit, could you return unused merchandise to the company for a refund? To see what opportunities are available, check out Web sites such as directsalescareers.com. Then get ready to hustle and sell as you've never hustled before because, as I said, the products will not sell themselves!

Party for a Profit

Wouldn't it be wonderful to host a party in which you made more money than you spent? Even if you are not involved with a direct-selling company like Mary Kay, you can still profit from the popularity of direct-selling home parties by having a bazaar party. Invite four to six vendors who represent distinctly different types of products to set up shop in your home for one evening. Make it clear that you expect to be compensated for the use of your home by receiving free merchandise or 20 percent of their sales for the night.

Make each seller responsible for inviting a group of potential customers to the party. Try to get a general idea of how many people are coming so you can arrange to have ample seating and food on hand. Invite at least one vendor who sells something food-related and can provide the appetizers. You as the hostess need only provide something to drink.

Create the ambience of an upscale boutique where every guest gets personal attention from the moment she enters the home. A cheerful greeter at the door sets the right tone from the start. Think about the flow of traffic, arranging intimate seating areas to encourage conversation, and the placement of tables for sellers. Display glossy brochures from all of the sellers on end tables and coffee tables throughout the party area. Be sure pets are safely tucked away behind closed doors away from allergic guests, and that your spouse and children are properly fed and warned about avoiding the party area. Nothing spoils the girlfriend get-together ambience faster than Junior raiding the fridge in his boxer shorts in full view of guests at the height of the party.

Stating what time the party ends on the invitation is just as important as stating what time the party starts. To signal the end of the party, casually turn off any background music and help the vendors pack up their tables. If some guests linger so long you fear they might take up permanent residence in your home, pleasantly ask if they had a good time and offer to get their coats for them, clearly implying the party is over.

Profiting from a Part-Time Job

No one has ever accused me of being a workaholic--a shopaholic maybe, but never a workaholic. However, there have been times when I worked two jobs for financial reasons, like when I bought a used car. I worked a full-time office job during the day that paid for basic living expenses like food, shelter, and cheap lip gloss. I also worked a part-time retail job in the evenings to help pay for the car loan. Frankly, the only thing worse than working one dead-end job is working two dead-end jobs. The minute my car loan was paid off, I dumped the part-time job and stayed out of debt by sticking with my full-time job and living within my means.

There are many reasons for getting a part-time job besides paying off a loan. The right part-time job can save you money in the form of employee discounts. When buying expensive items, like furniture, an extra percentage off the sale price can add up to real savings. As an employee, you'll know when the sales are scheduled to start, so you can take advantage of the best deals first.

An ideal second job would be one that gives you experience that relates to a career that genuinely interests you. If you are considering becoming an interior designer, for example, you might get a second job at the type of home decor store that attracts interior designers. That helps you develop customer service skills and gives you a chance to talk to designers about what it's really like to do what they do for a living. After being exposed to the less glamorous side of interior design, you might either decide that interior design is not for you, or use the experience to become better prepared for the day when you do become an interior designer.

You don't have to wait for the perfect part-time job to come along--create your own. With a little luck and a lot of initiative you can profit from the things you are passionate about. For example, if you love gardens or there is an area full of historical architecture near you, research the flora or buildings' history and start doing walking tours, guiding tour groups along and sharing your knowledge. Collaborating with the local tourist board or parks and recreation center may be helpful. Other possible part-time jobs include classroom teaching or one-on-one tutoring. Teach a language at a local travel agency and cash in on your knowledge of different cultures. Get paid to be the life of the party by teaching kid-friendly crafts at children's birthday parties. Act as an image consultant, teaching people how to shop smart and buy clothes that are appropriate for their figures and personal styles. There are far too many creative possibilities to name here.

Advertising your services on craigslist.com is a cheap way to promote yourself. The cost for your services ultimately depends on your level of skill and market demand.

Pick your part-time job with a sense of strategy. It should serve a specific purpose, such as paying off a debt, increasing your savings to a certain dollar amount, expanding your job skills, or testing the waters to see if your hobby has the potential to turn into a profitable career.

Simple Financial Strategies

A Whole Latte Nonsense

Financial gurus often promote the idea of deprivation as a solution to budget shortfalls, telling their audience to write up a detailed budget and cut back on the "frivolous" expenses, such as lattes. Their attitude is, "Just put the latte down and no one will get hurt." They may be able to survive on tap water, but depriving us latte lovers of our daily dose of caffeine and sugar could definitely result in someone (like these financial gurus) getting hurt.

Budgets are often too focused on the sacrifice of personal pleasure. Why not focus on spending less money on things that don't bring you pleasure? Using what I call "the pleasure principle victory journal" you can cut spending on practical things without giving up the vices that keep you sane and happy. There is no pesky budgeting spotlighting the fact that you'd rather invest in cute shoes than your IRA. Keeping a victory journal is simple--just do at least one financially savvy thing every week and record it in a notebook. Check out The Dollar Stretcher at stretcher.com for tons of great money saving ideas.

The easiest way to cut back financially is to stop spending money on things you don't use. Extra features on your phone or other services are good examples. Electronics still use electricity when plugged in, even if they are not on. Pull the plug for things that are not in use or used for short periods of time. Use less air conditioning or heat when you are away at work, and close the air vents in rooms that are rarely used.

Disposable items are a costly convenience. Instead of spending money on the same items over and over again, buy reusable items. Try buying plastic containers instead of disposable zipper bags. Do you really need to fill your bathroom trash can with used cotton balls, or would a soft, washable cloth work just as well?

Instead of sacrificing your vices, get a better deal on them. Take advantage of frequent-buyer cards that offer a free drink or meal. Get on your favorite stores' mailing lists for coupons. Buy snacks at the grocery store for less than they cost out of the vending machine. Charge your indulgence to the credit card that has the best rewards program.

At the end of the month sit down and review your progress. Just imagine yourself sitting there with a smug smile on your face, your victory journal in one hand and a double latte in the other.

The Benefits of Multiple Credit Cards

Using multiple credit cards is a simple way to get a clearer picture of where your money is going. To keep track of your spending, try using two or three widely recognized credit cards like Visa, MasterCard, or Discover, assigning different types of expenses to different credit cards. For example, putting only entertainment related expenses--such as magazine subscriptions, movies, concerts, cable, or music downloads--on one credit card shows you how much of your income is going towards entertainment. Another approach would be to use one credit card for online purchases and a different credit card for brick and mortar stores.

If someone steals your credit card information to make purchases, assigning different credit cards to different types of expenses helps to identify where it happened. If the credit card that was used illegally was one you used only in restaurants, for example, you will know to start eating at different restaurants. If dining at a restaurant where someone may have stolen your credit card information is still more appealing than doing your own cooking, you can always pay cash.

A home-based business calls for its own credit card even if it's a part-time business. Don't combine business related expenses such as supplies, promotional materials, and postage with your personal expenses. Having one credit card strictly for business expenses makes it easier to identify and report those expenses when doing your taxes. To get a more accurate idea of how much money you are really making from your business, just add up your sales for the month, then deduct your monthly credit card bill from your sales. The monthly total will either be delightful or depressing, but at least you'll know where you stand financially.

For all those financial advisers who insist that everyone keep one credit card for emergencies and put the rest through the shredder, I would like to point out that no one credit card is accepted everywhere. Having at least two different credit cards increases chances that one of them will be accepted.

The Sunny Side of Savings

Solar power saves you money in a variety of ways. For starters, using electronic devices that draw their power from solar batteries instead of an electric wall socket cuts down on your electric bill.

One of the most resourceful uses of solar power I've heard of was a homeowner who bought hanging outdoor solar lights that can be found at hardware stores or the lawn and garden section of mass retailers. He hung the solar powered lights in his windows during the day while he was at work. When he came home he put the solar lights in frequently used rooms, never bothering to turn his house lights on. By repeating the process of putting solar lights in the window to charge every day he dramatically reduced his electric bill.

Solar chargers for batteries, mobile phones, and digital cameras cut down your electric bill and may also extend the life of your batteries. Certain types of solar chargers have the added advantage of being portable enough to take on long road trips. A fully charged MP3 player is a real sanity saver when you are way out of range of your favorite music station.

Solar powered flashlights and calculators are just two examples of electronic devices that save money by eliminating the need to buy and replace batteries. Solar powered calculators can be found at office supply stores or mass retailers, while hardware stores or stores that sell camping equipment are good bets for finding solar powered flashlights.

The kind of money-saving solar power I am interested in is the budget-friendly kind that doesn't require me to strap surfboard-size sheets of solar panels to the side of my home. Thanks to solar powered devices that work in my home instead of being strapped to my home, I now have a sunny disposition toward solar power.

Understanding the True Cost of Things

The true cost of an item is what you ultimately end up paying for the item, not what it says on the price tag. What initially looks like a bargain might turn out to be an expensive mistake. To spare yourself the trauma of post-purchase sticker shock, ask yourself a few key questions before making that purchase.

What are the immediate costs for the item? Are there shipping or handling fees involved or taxes to consider? Free shipping may be available only on certain items. Amazon, for example, offers free shipping for many orders over $25, but this offer does not necessarily apply to other companies or individuals who are selling their merchandise through the amazon.com Web site. Be aware that online merchants charge sales tax, just as brick and mortar stores do.

Does it come with everything you need? A frugal friend of mine thought she was getting a great deal on a laptop computer only to find out after she bought it that it didn't include some of the commonly used Microsoft programs she just assumed were already programmed into the computer. Buying these programs brought her total cost up to the regular price of basic non-bargain laptop. Electronic items are notorious for needing new batteries and enough accessories to fill a Radio Shack. Do some research before whipping out your wallet.

What is the cost of maintaining the item? Is it a piece of equipment that will require routine maintenance and replacement parts? Can the item be cleaned and maintained, or will it have to be completely replaced once it is damaged or wears out? I once saw a care label in an expensive evening dress that said, "Do not hand wash, machine wash or dry clean." This dress was essentially designed to be used once and then disposed of, which is odd since the dress wasn't made out of paper towels. Buying a disposable dress is obviously a lot more expensive than buying a dress that has to be dry-cleaned but can be worn again.

What is the total cost of the item after it is completely paid for? When you think of credit card debt as one lump sum and don't think about how much individual items are really costing, it's easy to fool yourself into thinking that you are getting a better deal than you really are. No matter how much of a bargain something is at the time you buy it, if your credit card doesn't get paid off at the end of the month, then the cost of that item increases over time because you are now paying interest on that item. Buying smart means paying attention to the real cost of things so you don't end up paying more than you expect.

You've Got Mail!

Sometimes junk mail makes me laugh--like the one from a company that sent me a check for $5. The catch was that if I cashed the check I would automatically be signed up for fees and services costing $89! I did not cash the check. What I did was start thinking about the real costs of junk mail. It costs valuable time to go through it all. It opens you up to identity theft--credit card offers especially--and a lot of trees are wasted just so cynical consumers like me can roll their eyes at the latest junk mail scam before feeding anything with their names and addresses on it into the paper shredder.

To save time and a few trees you can register free online at the Direct Marketing Association (dmachoice.org) to be removed from junk mail lists. To stop preapproved credit card or insurance offers and reduce your chances of identity theft, call 888-567-8688 or go to optoutprescreen.com which is affiliated with major consumer credit reporting companies. If catalogs are a shopping weakness or just a nuisance, contact catalogchoice.org to stop the flow of unwanted catalogs.

One of the most annoying junk mail promotions I have seen is the fake friend promotion. Someone sends you what appears to be a copy of a newspaper article about a product with a handwritten note addressing you by your first name with a personal note about how the sender thought of you when he or she found out about this product. What appears to be a photocopied article sent by a caring friend (a friend with a questionable or nonexistent return address) is actually a mass-produced brochure sent out by a complete stranger plugging the product in the article. If you want to keep your money and lose a "friend," contact dmachoice.org today!

How to Avoid Common Retail Rip-offs

Head Games That Cost You Money

Reading store signs and sale tags is kind of like reading a mystery novel. Things are not always what they seem, and if you're not careful, your finances could become a victim of foul play. Shut the book on overspending right now by learning how to recognize deceptive tactics.

Take end caps, for example. At a grocery store a display at the end of an aisle is packed with merchandise with the price of the merchandise displayed boldly on eye-catching signs. It's on the end, and the price is prominently featured, so it must be on sale, right? Not necessarily. Unless the sign specifically indicates that the item is on sale or a part of some sort of special, then it is probably at the regular price. Never assume something is on sale.

Another way retailers mislead customers into thinking that they are getting a great deal is price matching. Retailers post signs saying that they will match competitor's prices on identical items. Customers see the price matching sign and assume that the store they are in must have the lowest prices overall. The retailers that post these signs may carry merchandise that is more expensive across the board than their competitors, but they know many customers will not take the time to compare the prices of the items they are buying.

One deceptive retail tactic is what I call "bargains by association." For example, a store known for low prices puts a special display of microwaves in the middle of a main aisle close to the home appliance section. The price for this prominently displayed microwave is ridiculously cheap. The customer decides he wants a different style of microwave with more features than the cheap, no-frills one displayed in the main aisle. The customer heads to the appliance section, thinking that the other microwaves must be bargains as well. The retailer has implanted the idea that it has the lowest prices by prominently displaying one item that is a real bargain next to similar, more desirable items at prices that may be higher than the competition's.

The best way to avoid falling for these head games is to verify that you are getting a good deal by paying close attention to the signs on products and comparing prices among sellers online before heading out to shop for more expensive items. There are countless price comparison Web sites out there. Using Google or another online search engine, type the words "price comparison" and the name of the item you are shopping for to bring up a list of the most current and popular comparison Web sites. Create your own happy ending for every shopping venture by avoiding assumptions and paying close attention to prices.

'As Advertised' Promotions Mislead Customers

There are two rules I live by as a Cheap Diva: Always pay attention to numbers, and always read the fine print. With "as advertised" promotions you have to do both. A newspaper advertisement promoting skin care products caught my eye. The ad mentioned two types of body lotions that were on sale. On the same page that mentioned the sale items, the ad went on to list other products by the same brand.

I went to the store expecting to get a sale price on a body wash that was mentioned in the advertisement. The product display showed the sale prices for the two lotions mentioned in the ad as being on sale, but the other products had "as advertised" promotional tags next to them with no mention of a discount or sale price. This made me suspicious. A closer inspection of the price sticker on the shelf of the "as advertised" item revealed that the item was selling at regular price.

I realized that the only thing "as advertised" means is that the item or brand was mentioned in an advertisement. The fact that the products were featured in the same advertisement and they were the same brand as the sale items featured gave the misleading impression that the items I wanted were on sale. I was so annoyed I didn't buy the item. I decided to save my cash for a real deal and not buy into misleading advertising. After that, I made a point of looking for the words "sale" or "clearance" on signs and ignoring the words "as advertised."

Don't Lose Cash When a Store Closes

With retail stores shutting down faster than you can say "I wonder if they're having any good store closing sales?" we really need to pay attention to how we spend our money. The now closed Sharper Image store offers a perfect example of why cold, hard cash may be a better gift than a gift certificate. I heard on the news that the stores were selling gift certificates right up until the day the store closed. No one bothered to tell customers that they needed to spend the gift certificate immediately because in 24 hours it wasn't going to be worth the paper it was printed on. If you buy a gift certificate and the store goes out of business, the gift certificate becomes worthless and you have no way to get your money back.

I learned another valuable lesson with a buyer-beware theme straight from another local news segment. A man who was remodeling his kitchen went to purchase some granite countertops that were advertised for a great price. When he went to the store, the overeager salesperson not only honored the advertised price but kept dropping the price to sweeten the deal. Thinking he was getting a great deal, the customer spent more than $1,000 on granite countertops that were supposed to be shipped in from another location. Unfortunately the company's financial status wasn't as solid as its countertops. It went out of business within a week of the customer placing his order, and he never got the countertops. The good news is that he had used a credit card to make the purchase, so he was only obligated to pay his credit card company $50 of the total. By using a credit card he ended up losing $50 instead of the more than $1,000 he would have lost had he paid with cash or a check.

I bought my TV at an electronics store that sold nothing but televisions. The sales staff tried to make me spend an additional $40 on an extended warranty. They told me that if nothing went wrong with the TV and I didn't use the warranty after a certain period of time I could apply that $40 toward another purchase. I said no to the extended warranty. Most problems with electronic devices happen within the first two years, while they are still under the manufacturer's warranty, so I never buy an extended warranty. At the time I felt good about not spending an additional $40. I felt even better about my decision about a year or so later when the store closed, which would have made the store warranty useless.

At the risk of stating the obvious, you should only buy stuff you are sure you really want. The sales receipt may say that you have 90 days to return the item, but the sales receipt doesn't come with any guarantee that the store will be in business in 90 days. Store closings are a fact of life even in good economic times. Shop smart, and you won't have to worry about store closings leaving you empty-handed.

Hang Onto Your Handbag

The most important shopping companion a woman can take with her is her handbag. Most likely the bag contains cash, a portable phone, and the keys to her castle. Losing a handbag can be a hassle, so do yourself a favor and always keep it close to you when shopping. Leaving your purse under a pile of clothes in the dressing room while you go back out into the store to shop is an open invitation to thieves. While you're grabbing another cute blouse to try on, a thief can easily grab your bag and walk away unnoticed.

If you need to leave the dressing room for better lighting or a three-way mirror in the public part of the store, keep your handbag in your hand. If your bag is bulkier than carry-on luggage, just set it down between you and the mirror. The mirror shows you who is around you, and a thief would have to walk directly in front of you to steal your bag.

Before switching to office jobs, I worked at various home décor and women's clothing stores as a salesperson. During one of my retail shifts there was an incident in which a woman walked up to a customer who had an open handbag, engaged in some friendly chitchat with the customer, and stole the customer's wallet from her bag right in front of her!

The best handbag is one with a long strap that leaves your hands free for snapping up bargains and reduces the risk that you will absentmindedly set it down somewhere. Never leave your handbag in a shopping cart unattended while your attention is focused on something else, like scoping out new merchandise. Even if you only turn your back for a second, that's still enough time for a thief to grab your bag from your shopping cart and disappear. For the record, I have never had my handbag stolen. By using these strategies I have made myself an inconvenient target for thieves looking for easy money.

Shopping Strategies That Really Pay Off

Online Versus In-Store Shopping

There are pros and cons to shopping for clothes online. One of the biggest pros is that you can shop in your pajamas and fuzzy slippers without getting strange looks from sales clerks. The biggest con is that you can't see the merchandise up close and feel the fabric to see what you are really getting. For fashion lovers who shop regularly for clothes that are a bit more upscale than a $7 Target T-shirt, a strategic approach to shopping is to combine online with in-store shopping.

If you prefer to hit the stores in person to see the merchandise up close and personal, it's still worth checking out your favorite store's Web site to see if there are any in-store sales or offers you need to be aware of. Some stores feature special sales and promotions that are only good online. Online promotions may also include printable coupons that you can take with you for in-store purchases.

Shopping in stores reveals what an online photograph can't. You can feel the weight of the fabric, hold the piece up next to you to check out length, and see the true color of the item. Every computer screen shows color a little differently, so that "spice" color shirt that looks so chic on the computer screen may actually be pumpkin orange in real life. Shopping in stores also takes the guesswork out of which size to buy, because you have an opportunity to try it on, or simply look it over to make an educated guess at the size and fit.

Before you buy, check the price. Is it on sale? If it is on sale, is it a *real* sale or was the original price so inflated that the so-called sale price just drops the price to one a customer would realistically be willing to pay? If the price doesn't impress you as being a good deal, write down the garment information for future reference. A small notepad is a shopping essential. Information to take note of includes the name of the store, the original price, the fiber content, and the name of the collection (stores will often assign names like "City Style Pant" to a pair of simple black pants to make them seem more like a style statement than a wardrobe basic). You will be happy to have this information when you find yourself staring at a store's Web site that has multiple styles of black pants, all of which look alike. As you go through your favorite stores, keep making notes of anything you would seriously consider purchasing.

So why hit the Web after taking the time to hit the mall? To save money and get the right size. Cute clothes tend to disappear quickly when they go on sale. By the time the items you want go on sale, the retail store might be out of your size, while the online store should have a more in-depth stock of different sizes. To be notified of store sales you can sign up to get e-mail notices from that store.

The time between when you are in the store and when you are shopping online also provides a cooling-off period that reduces the impulse to buy something immediately. By taking the time to see what you already have in your closet and compare it against your shopping wish list, you can see whether the pieces you are thinking about buying are filling gaps in your wardrobe or if they are repeats of things you already have.

Making a list of things you want to buy and taking a look inside your closet also help you prioritize. Without the pressure of having to make a shopping decision on the spot, you can calmly look at your list and see which pieces within your budget stand out as "must haves." You might end up buying one of the more expensive pieces, but by shopping both online and in stores you can feel confident that you are buying the right piece.

Life in the Express Lane

As a former retail saleswoman, I like to think of myself as something of a shopping expert. When I am in line at the checkout lane behind the inevitable "problem" customer who is holding up the line and making time stand still, I just think about how I would never be that shopper. This feeling of smug superiority lasts just until the mortifying moment when something happens to make me the much-loathed clog in the machinery of the checkout express lane.

The last time this happened, the cashier was ringing up a bag of apples and the bar code on the bag was not registering in the computer. The cashier flipped the bag down on one side, then the other. The bag landed with such a hard, thunking sound every time she flipped it I was starting to get concerned that I was about to have a bag of applesauce on my hands. I finally noticed the small plastic tie at the top of the bag had a small bar code about half the size of the bar code printed on the bag. I pointed this out to the cashier, and she was able to ring the apples up before flipping them into a pulp.

Here are a few tips for the sake of your produce and your sanity to get through the checkout lane faster: Check the item before you put it in the cart for some sort of bar code. If the item does not have a tag with a bar code, find a nearly identical item that has a bar code and bring it to the register with you. Explain to the cashier that you just want to buy item A, but it didn't have a tag, so you brought item B to the register so it could be rung up. One cashier was so impressed when I did this that she happily pointed out my resourcefulness to another cashier.

Know the price of the items you are buying. Sometimes a sale sign on a rack will look as if it applies to the item you are buying, but read the sign carefully to be sure. Signs or merchandise can mysteriously end up in the wrong place. It's quite a disappointment to get to the register to find out the item you had your heart set on is not, in fact, 75 percent off.

If the item you are buying is featured in an advertisement, have that advertisement with you when you get to the cash register. Watch the screen on the cash register to be sure you are paying the price you should be paying. If the price rings up incorrectly, you can show the cashier the advertisement and save him or her the trouble of doing a price check.

Have coupons ready to hand the cashier before the items have been totaled. Better yet, have your money ready to pay for your merchandise before it's totaled. Nothing is more annoying to people standing in line than the customer with a bewildered look on her face digging around in her purse as if it never occurred to her that she would actually have to pay for her stuff.

Now that you have paid for your items and gotten a receipt, move on! This is not the time to balance your checkbook or reorganize your purse. Step aside to take care of these personal tasks and give someone else a chance to hold up the line.

Sign Up to Save Money

I have one simple criterion for giving out personal information to cashiers, retailers, or anyone else requesting personal information: What's in it for me? I will gladly give out my address (never my home phone number) to a few stores that I frequent, like ULTA or Bed Bath & Beyond, that regularly send out coupons to customers who sign up for their mailing lists. Sale notices from high priced luxury stores would only be of interest to me if I won the lottery.

Another way to get the inside scoop on sales is signing up with retailers or Web sites to be notified by e-mail of current sales. With Google e-mail you don't have to give out a lot of personal information. You can create a free e-mail account with Google using only your first initial and middle name, for example. Creating an e-mail account just for promotional e-mails prevents sale e-mails from cluttering up your personal e-mail account.

The problem with signing up for sale notices from your favorite stores is that they e-mail you about every single sale practically every week. It gets annoying when you are waiting for a particular item to go on sale and the e-mails that keep popping up in your inbox announce sales on everything and anything except the one item you actually want. To find out about sales on the things you want, sign up with a helpful shopping Web site like Shop It To Me (shopittome.com). Sign up for free, pick items that interest you from hundreds of well-known brands, and Shop It To Me will send you a sale notice via e-mail only when items from the brands you chose go on sale. Being alerted to sales on the items you are interested in is a real time saver as well as a money saver.

If you don't want retailers giving out your personal information to third parties (other businesses they sell customer information to), look for some sort of box on the sign-up form that gives you the option of not disclosing your information. For those situations when a cashier asks me to provide a home phone or zip code where there's no real incentive for me to do so, such as receiving coupons, I politely decline by saying I don't give out that information. What I don't say is that the request for personal information didn't pass the "What's in it for me?" test.

Add Coupons to Your Shopping List

I've always been good at collecting coupons. Unfortunately I haven't always been good about using those coupons before they expired. After throwing away countless expired coupons over the years I finally came up with the brilliant idea that I should go through my coupons whenever I make a shopping list. If I am going to the grocery store, for example, I grab my coupon stash from my purse and pull out any grocery related coupons.

If I have a coupon for peanut butter I will make a point of including peanut butter on my shopping list. After all of the grocery items that I have coupons for have been added to my shopping list, I fold the list in half like a file folder and tuck the coupons I want to use inside the list.

Coupons can be a great savings tool, but they often apply towards the more expensive brands. When I get to the store I compare the price of the generic store brand cereal against the price of a popular name brand cereal, for example. If the generic cereal is cheaper than the cereal I have a coupon for, even after deducting the coupon from the price, I buy the generic cereal. After all, shopping smart isn't just about clipping coupons; it's about getting the best price, period.

Save Money at Going-Out-of-Business Sales

Going out of business may be sad for the retailer going through it, but it's an event that appeals to savvy shoppers eager to snap up great deals. If you don't happen to catch the latest store closings from your preferred news source, hitting the local strip malls and your favorite stores frequently increases your odds of discovering a going-out-of-business sale and snapping up the good stuff before it disappears. Going out of business means that all sales are final, so carry cash, and if you are buying electronics, have the sales associate plug the item into an electrical outlet to make sure it works before you buy it.

The signs may be screaming "Going out of business!" and "Everything must go!" but you still need to pay attention to price and quality, just as you would any other sale. I went to one going-out-of-business sale for a furniture store where the "original" prices were so inflated, and the quality of the merchandise so poor, that even at 70 percent off I wasn't tempted to buy a thing. It was certainly no mystery as to why they were going out of business.

Some going-out-of-business sales start their markdowns off at a measly 20 percent off, which is not much of a discount.

In one case a store actually increased the price of its merchandise right before the sale. Management knew customers would assume they were getting a good deal simply because the store was going out of business.

Don't limit your shopping at a going-out-of-business sale to regular merchandise. I have a beautiful Art Deco mannequin head that I display on a pedestal like a sculpture. I got a terrific deal on this distinctive display piece at a going-out-of-business sale for a women's clothing store. Other items to keep your eyes open for are tables, display and shelving units that could be used at home, and dress forms that serve as stylish home decor.

Treasure Hunting in Thrift Stores

Thrift stores are best appreciated by shoppers who are willing to wade through racks of cheap, tacky clothes just for the thrill of finding a truly fabulous piece in nearly new condition among all the fashion rejects. To quickly identify goods that have hardly, if ever, been worn, follow these tips.

- Check for smells and stains. There is no guarantee you will be able to get rid of either one of these, so it's better to hold out for clean-looking, odor-free items.
- Look for an excessive amount of pills on the fabric. This indicates the item has been worn frequently.
- Look for fabrics that aren't ripped, puckered at the seams or extremely limp. Faded or limp clothing has probably been washed and worn frequently.

- Look at the care label. If it is crisp, with sharp printing that shows no signs of fading, this suggests that the item has probably been seldom washed and worn.
- The whole "ick" factor of wearing used shoes shouldn't prevent you from at least looking at the shoe rack. Some shoes are donated without ever being worn. Look for shoes that have no odor. Also see if their shape is distorted in any way from being worn, or if they look as though they just came out of a shoe box. It's a good sign if there are no signs of wear on the heel of the shoe.
- When looking at handbags, check the inside lining for tears, and check the outside for scratches and rips in the material. Set the bag on something flat, like a shelf or table, to see whether the shape of the bag has been distorted through use.

Some thrift stores either don't have dressing rooms, or their dressing rooms may be occupied when you need them. Dress in a way that allows you to try on clothes without a dressing room and without being arrested for indecent exposure. Wear a dress or skirt to try on pants or a skirt on under your own clothes. Or wear something fitted so you can try on things over your clothing. Not all thrift stores accept credit cards, so be prepared to pay in cash. Happy hunting!

Shopping Strategies for Craft Shows and Flea Markets

For the serious bargain hunter, scouring flea markets, craft shows, and garage sales for treasures is serious business, requiring both skill and strategy. For the not so serious bargain hunter, treasure hunting is an excuse to enjoy some fun in the sun while keeping an eye open for interesting finds. Either way, it makes for a more pleasant experience if you come prepared.

First, do a little homework, so you have a general idea of what to expect. Check local print publications, usually found at the public library, or local news and entertainment Web sites for current craft shows and sales. Look for details in the ads about who is selling what. If it's a craft show or flea market, is it being held in a big outdoor area to accommodate lots of vendors, or is it a smaller, more intimate craft show with fewer vendors? Your friends may have ideas about where to go, or ask people who operate local antique shops if they know of any good flea markets or craft shows.

Dress for comfort and protection. Supportive walking shoes that cover enough of the foot to offer protection against rough terrain and solid concrete are a must. A wide-brim hat and sunglasses offer protection and let you discreetly eye the merchandise before making your move. Keep your cool by wearing clothing made of breathable fabrics like cotton. If the weather is cool, wear layers, like lightweight sweaters, that can be removed if you start to overheat from all that intense bargain hunting. Extremely lightweight fabrics offer little in the way of sun protection, so slather on a layer of heavy-duty sunscreen under your clothes before heading out.

A few good things to have on hand include a small notebook and pen, a phone or other portable device with Internet access, and a bottle of water to wash down all those energy bars you packed to keep you going. Carry lots of cash in smaller bills, since sellers, like the craft show queen selling bottle-cap jewelry, may not be prepared to take credit cards.

Arrive at your destination early in a vehicle that will accommodate what you are most likely to buy. If buying furniture is a possibility, drive a vehicle that will have enough space to transport it, or go with a friend who has a more spacious car. Measure the part of the vehicle you intend to use for transporting your finds and record these measurements in a small notebook. You can compare the size of the space against the measurements of a potential purchase before trying to squeeze your fabulous find into a vehicle that doesn't have room for it.

Some craft shows and flea markets are so big it's easy to forget where you saw what. If you have your eye on something but are not ready to make a purchase, make a note of the item, the price, and its location in your notebook. If you fall in love with an item but you have a lot more looking to do and don't want to drag it all over the place, ask the sellers if they will hold it for you. If they won't hold it without a commitment, go ahead and pay for it (making sure you get a receipt) with the understanding that you will pick it up later.

With so much stuff for sale you will inevitably come across things you never knew existed and for which you have no idea what a fair price would be. When a smooth-talking vendor claims you are getting a great deal for his precious wares, call him on it. Whip out your portable electronic device with Internet access and see what items similar in make and condition to the one you are looking at are selling for on Web sites such as eBay. Most important, have fun! Enjoy the great outdoors! Enjoy the company of your shopping companions and sellers, and enjoy the thrill of the hunt!

The Art of Window-Shopping

While I can often be found stalking the aisles of places like Target in search of cheap chic, I also frequent upscale retail stores looking for the one thing the bargain stores don't provide: inspiration. The more expensive the merchandise, the more likely it is that somewhere along the line a professional display person or stylist has gotten his or her creative hands on it, and the results are worth a closer look.

Lower priced stores sell merchandise; higher priced stores sell a vision. Higher priced stores display pieces in relationship to each other. Instead of just sticking rows of dishes on a shelf, they create entire displays with fully set tables including coordinating items such as napkins, silverware, and centerpieces. The goal is to create such a gorgeously tempting display that the customer forgets all the other tableware jammed in their dining-room cabinet and starts fantasizing about entertaining in a very coordinated, Martha Stewart-like manner.

The good news is this coordinated vision can be applied to just about any budget. When a home decor display or a mannequin striking a pose catches your eye, take a moment to study the different pieces of the display to see how they relate to one another. Look at how the placement of objects in furniture and accessories could be applied to your own home. Take a look at what colors are used together and how they are used. Brightly colored pillows are often shown on a neutral sofa to add a dash of vibrant color against the more subdued background of the sofa.

While you're taking lessons in design, make note of combinations of materials and textures. Shiny objects such as metal jewelry are often combined with duller fabrics. The contrast accentuates the glossy surface of the metal. Another design element used to great effect is proportion. Mannequins sporting bold prints on their clothing demand bold-scale jewelry that will complement the print without being overwhelmed by it. Now that you have tons of ideas to inspire and inform your design sense, hit the local Crate & Barrel, Target, and Wal-Mart to stock up on cheap-chic knockoffs of all the fabulous items you drooled over at the high-end stores.

How to Buy Gifts without Going Broke

A Valuable Guide to Savvy Gift Giving

During the holiday season a lot of money is wasted on gifts the recipients may not need or want. Sometimes when the recipient of a gift utters the phrase, "Oh, you shouldn't have!" he or she really means it. What's worse is that the unlucky recipient may get stuck with the gift. Many stores will not accept a return without a receipt and all the original tags attached. If the store does offer a store credit, it will be for the current selling price (the item is probably on clearance by now), not the price the buyer paid for it.

A good shopping strategy will help you avoid a variety of gift giving mistakes: Save your gift receipts in an envelope. If the item goes on sale before you give it to the recipient, call the store to find out whether, if you take the item and the receipt to the store, they will give you a credit or cash for the difference.

No one likes to think of having a gift returned, but just in case a big fluffy pink sweater with white elephants parading across the bust is not what the recipient wanted (yes, I actually did receive this fashion abomination as a gift), get a gift receipt from the cashier when paying for the item. A gift receipt has the bar code for the item printed on it, but not the price of the item. Leave all tags and labels on the item. You can cross out the price, but leave the bar code intact.

Buy gifts you plan on mailing far enough in advance so you can choose the cheapest shipping method. If you are ordering an item from a Web site or catalog, the earlier you order the item, the better your chances of getting it on time. If the item is going to be delayed, you can usually find out far enough ahead of time to make other arrangements.

Many gifts can be sent in a standard envelope with the only shipping cost being a regular stamp. Gifts that fit inside an envelope include tickets to a local sporting or entertainment event; gift certificates for movies, theatres, restaurants, and local spas; magazine subscriptions; phone cards; and online gift certificates for retail Web sites.

Spend as little as possible on gift wrap so more of your money can go toward the gift itself. Gift bags of various sizes can be found at a dollar store for $1 apiece! Maybe that's why they call it the dollar store. While you're at the dollar store, keep an eye open for coordinating tissue paper to fill all those bargain bags.

Buying in Multiples Saves Money on Gifts

Sure it's supposed to be the thought that counts, but when it comes to gifts why not put as much thought into getting the best deal as you do into the gift itself? Buying in multiples is one way to save money on gifts.

Cosmetic bag sets with three or four bags can easily be broken up to give different glamour gals on your gift list their own bags. The bags often end up being such a great deal that when you break up the set, you should have enough money left over to fill each one with beauty bargains chosen especially for the recipients.

Keep an eye open for any kind of set that can easily be broken up. Sets of clear or plain white glass or ceramic bowls with lids that can be used in the microwave and oven and are also freezer safe can be separated and filled with different kinds of food for different recipients. Chips and gourmet dip could fill a large bowl for one person, spiced nuts go in a different bowl, and cookies in yet another bowl for various people on your gift list.

Save some cash by stocking up. For one candle lover on my gift list, I bought about a dozen scented votive candles to take advantage of the quantity discount a retailer offered. I selected candles that smelled like cookies and other yummy baked goods, then I put the candles in a cookie tin to carry out the sweets theme.

Small quantities can offer great deals, too. One of my best deals was a buy-one-get-one-free offer for body lotions from Bath & Body Works. I knew one of my friends loved their lotions, so I bought one bottle for her and got a free one for myself. When you get great deals, it suddenly becomes possible to add yourself to your gift list.

Save Cash with Eco-Friendly Gift Ideas

During the holidays too much money is spent on wrapping materials that get tossed into the trash faster than expired eggnog. This holiday season cut down on wasteful spending and waste in general by cutting down on gift-related costs like shipping and packaging materials.

For the tuned-in, tech savvy people on your gift list, an Amazon (amazon.com) or iTunes (apple.com) gift certificate is the perfect gift. It provides them with hours of entertainment without using materials and resources like a CD or DVD. With a gift certificate, they can download a mind-boggling variety of music or other media to their preferred media players.

For a more low-tech gift, try something handmade. Instead of throwing out perfectly good peanut butter jars when they are empty, use them as containers for gifts. Hold a hair dryer about 6 inches from the jar to remove the paper label, and wash the jar with soapy water. When the lid is dry, glue a piece of fabric to the top part of the lid. Let about an inch of fabric drape over the sides of the jar, and tie a ribbon around the lid. Fill the jar with hand-dipped chocolate pretzels or some other tempting goody. Now wrap your handiwork in a cloth napkin. Set the filled jar in the middle of the napkin and bring the corners of the napkin straight up. Tie the ends of the napkins together right above the lid of the jar with a piece of ribbon. Every part of this gift is reusable or consumable in some way, so aside from ruining the recipient's diet, it's a gift you can feel good about giving.

Whenever possible, try to make the packaging for the gift an essential part of the gift. A pajama outfit tucked inside a pillowcase made of organic fabric and tied at the opening with a hair ribbon is a cute and practical gift. Decorative boxes, such as cookie tins and the kind of hat boxes you find at Hobby Lobby, don't require any additional wrapping and are more likely to end up being used for storage than in the trash. If you are a fan of eBay you can find tons of hat boxes, cookie tins, and similar containers in mint condition for cheap prices.

Some people on your shopping list don't need new stuff to add to the pile of stuff they already have and don't know what to do with. Why not give the people you enjoy spending time with the gift of a shared experience? There are usually plenty of affordable holiday-themed decorated home tours and other entertaining events for shoppers on a Scrooge-like budget. If you normally spent about $20 a person on a certain group of style-savvy people, for example, you could buy tickets to a decorated homes tour that costs $20 or less per person for your friends. Buying the tickets in bulk may entitle you to special discounts.

Give the tickets to your stylish pals along with an invitation. Invite them to get together to enjoy the homes tour at a time that is convenient for everyone. Arrange for your friends to meet at your home so you can carpool. You could provide cocoa and other hot beverages and snacks at your home after everyone has enjoyed the tour or, if your holiday budget makes you feel more like a Scrooge than Santa Claus, you can suggest that everyone meet at a coffee shop after the tour.

The holiday season can sometimes be more stressful than joyous. Why not skip the whole business of buying and exchanging new gifts during the busy holiday season? Give your friends and family a break and host a white elephant gift exchange after the holidays. Each guest brings, concealed in a plain bag, a gift they received that they don't want that is within a certain price range, say less than $20. Set all the gifts on a table in full view of your guests. Have guests draw numbers to see who gets to choose first. Everyone takes turns picking a gift. To make things a bit more interesting, allow guests keep the wrapped gift they just selected from the table or "steal" a gift from another guest when it's their turn. The person who had a gift "stolen" can't steal it back but can steal a gift from someone who has already opened a gift, or choose an unwrapped gift from the table. To prevent total gift swapping chaos, limit guests to one steal per person. The stealing option turns the gift exchange into a spontaneous, fast-paced game.

>>>>>>>>>>>>>>>>>>><<<<<<<<<<<<<<<<<<<

Recommended Reading

The Green Year: 365 Small Things You Can Do to Make a Big Difference, by Jodi Helmer, is packed with the kind of eco-friendly tips that will leave you with more green in your wallet. The book offers one tip for every day of the year. Read this book, and you will discover that it really is easy being green.

>>>>>>>>>>>>>>>>>>><<<<<<<<<<<<<<<<<<<

Part Two: Fashion

"Fashion fades, style is eternal."

--Yves Saint Laurent

It's So You!

Creating a Signature Style

A signature style is all about you! It expresses your unique personality, flatters your figure and fits your budget. By dressing according to your own signature style, you tend to limit your purchases to what really works and avoid unflattering fashion fads that rob you of both spending money and closet space. A signature style can revolve around certain pieces, like funky accessories, or a total look based on certain colors, patterns, or the interesting way you mix pieces together.

The key to developing a signature style is discovering what versions of the things you love are going to work for your figure as well as your personality. Some are going to be more flattering than others, so be selective. I'm just wild about animal prints, especially leopard and tiger prints. I look for subdued background colors like brown or gray, and I look at the scale of the print. I check to see that the leopard spots are not so tiny and uniform they look like polka dots, or so big I look as if I belong in a Flintstones cartoon. While I might consider wearing a bold zebra print on a handbag or pair of shoes, I know that if I wore that same bold print on a shirt or skirt it would overwhelm my figure.

The difference between a signature style and a rut is that a signature style can be expressed in a variety of ways while still staying true to you. Brooches make a wonderful signature piece because they can be displayed in a variety of ways, acting as a pendant on a necklace one day and adorning a jacket lapel or headband the next.

Signature pieces can be ultra-trendy yet still affordable. If your signature piece is a fashion-forward handbag, buy a designer knockoff similar to the expensive version. Always buy from a reputable company that isn't trying to pass the copycat handbags off as the real deal. Whatever your signature piece is, you will be using it frequently, so buy the best quality you can afford, even when it's a designer knockoff.

For inspiration, look at magazines like *In Style*. Study mannequins in display windows to see how pieces are put together. Watch stylish movies and TV shows. Whether at work or play, take a look at the women around you for style inspiration. After considering all the possibilities, try on different looks and see what feels right to you.

Look More Polished with Less Effort

Presenting an image of effortless chic is easier than you might think. Clothes that fit properly with a silhouette that follows the lines of your body always look polished. A bit of stretchy Lycra in the fabric goes a long way toward helping the garment keep its shape for hours on end. Lycra is especially useful for keeping your bottom firm and your knees from bagging (I'm talking about the clothes here) in pants and jeans.

Nothing makes you look rumpled faster than wrinkles. For a preview of how well that cute top is going to look after you start wearing it, do a wrinkle test before you buy it. Grab a section of the fabric, crumple it in your hand, and hold it in your fist for about ten seconds. Release it and see how wrinkled it looks. Many fabrics will wrinkle eventually. The goal is to choose fabrics where wrinkles are less conspicuous. Fabrics with a permanently crinkled texture provide the perfect camouflage for wrinkles.

Wrinkles are less noticeable in printed fabric. The pattern distracts attention from the wrinkles by giving the eye something more interesting to focus on. Patterns are also terrific for disguising any stains that inconveniently appear when you are nowhere near a washer.

Looking polished should be a low-maintenance affair, no matter what type of event you are attending. Strapless tops that have to be routinely yanked up, shawls that are forever falling off your shoulder, or shoes that are outright painful after a whole ten minutes of wearing them distract you from enjoying yourself and the company of others. What you wear should make you feel fabulous, not self-conscious.

How you carry yourself is as much a part of your image as your clothes. Maintaining good posture is essential to projecting a sophisticated image. So keep your head up, shoulders slightly back, back comfortably erect and not hunched over, and walk like a lady, not a football quarterback charging down the field. Exercise programs based on dance moves, or any other type of exercise that emphasizes coordination and graceful movement, can help you stand tall and move through the world with a confident stride.

How to Create a Style Mix That Works

Mixing clothing pieces in a variety of ways to create more outfits without buying more stuff is a budget-friendly way to expand your wardrobe options. Of course, an outfit that mixes different pieces of your wardrobe together in an unexpected way has the potential to look fabulous or frightful. Trying too hard to come up with clever combinations can result in some truly regrettable fashion statements. Like the time fashion magazines were promoting the girlie/macho look consisting of a light, flowing summer dress accessorized with heavy biker boots. Instead of looking like a fashion plate, the model looked as if she was having an identity crisis.

To master the art of mixing different pieces of clothing, take a closer look at an attractive outfit that combines pieces that appear to be very different in nature. At first glance the pieces may not look as though they relate to each other, but by taking a closer look at design elements like texture, color, or silhouette, you will find that there is some common thread (no pun intended) that pulls the whole look together.

While I was flipping through a clothing catalog, an unexpected combo caught my attention. The model wore a plain pair of pants with a white cable-knit hooded sweater topped off with a black tailored jacket. At first an office-appropriate jacket paired with a sweater inspired by a hooded sweatshirt seemed like an odd combination, but it worked. The jacket and the sweater were the same level of formality. The medium-weight sweater with its figure-flattering, narrow cables was clearly a step above a typical sweatshirt. The tailored jacket was wool flannel, similar to a wool blanket, and gave off a slightly more casual vibe than a more tightly woven traditional suit fabric would have. Every piece of the outfit had the same slightly relaxed fit that followed the contours of the body but allowed for comfort and freedom of movement.

Mixing different patterns in the same outfit is tricky. The pattern mix that looks so chic on a runway model could easily be mistaken for a clown costume when worn by real women in the real world. One misconception that prevents women from mixing patterns more freely is assuming a pattern must be a graphic design that's printed on the surface of a fabric. Anything from the distinctive design or texture that's woven or knitted into a solid colored fabric to the open, lacy designs of a crocheted sweater could also be considered a pattern.

One of the most casual yet chic takes on pattern mixing I've seen was on a former coworker. She wore ballet flats in a brown leopard print with slim khaki pants (no unflattering pleats for her) and a long-sleeve T-shirt in a rich teal under a chocolate brown sweater crocheted in a lacey, open design that allowed the teal to show through. The unexpected pattern combination of the crocheted sweater and leopard print flats worked because the patterns weren't close enough to each other to clash. The dark brown in the leopard print of the flats coordinated nicely with the chocolate brown of the crocheted cardigan, while the teal T-shirt added a colorful complement to all those neutral browns. This clever combination showed me that an unexpected style mix can work in the real world, not just the fashion runway.

Shop Your Closet

In spite of lifestyle magazines featuring "must have" items that you simply must run out and buy right now in order for your life to be complete, many women are choosing to shop their own closets looking for fresh new ways to wear the pieces they already own.

To get started shopping your closet, separate tops and bottoms that fit properly into two groups. Pull out one top or bottom and try pairing it with different pieces. Start mixing the pieces you rarely or never wear with the pieces you wear often and see what happens. Lightweight fitted pieces such as knit T-shirts are perfect for layering and creating fresh looks. If certain pieces don't seem to go with anything at all, ask yourself if you really want them in your wardrobe. Would you rather sell or donate them to free up closet space? A lot of this coordinating can be done by simply hanging a skirt or pants on a doorknob and holding up different tops to see what works.

Complete the new outfits you have pulled together by adding accessories. Mix and match accessories in new ways. An easy way to coordinate accessories is color. A pair of vivid purple flats can easily work with an outfit that includes a royal blue top if the top and the shoes are the same intensity or brightness.

Consider repurposing some of your most stylish accessories to create a new look. A chain belt draped once or twice around the neck becomes a slinky necklace. An attractive neck scarf can be worn as anything from a belt to a headband to a halter top.

Keep mixing up, layering, and coordinating pieces until you are satisfied that you have tried everything that might work, or you are satisfied with the number of new outfits you have created. Record your sartorial success by taking pictures of the outfits that really work if that helps you remember what works with what. Ultimately, style is not about how much you have, it's what you do with what you have.

Versatile Accessories

Buying one well-designed piece of jewelry is better than buying a bunch of junky looking jewelry that cheapens the look of your outfits. You will look more stylish and get more use out of well-designed jewelry versatile enough to work with a variety of outfits. I am not suggesting that you run out right now and buy the world's most boring pair of pearl stud earrings just because they go with everything. Exotic designs that look like they came from faraway lands instead of your local Wal-Mart can be just as versatile as a simple string of pearls. Part of what makes a piece versatile is proportion. If it looks like you have hubcaps hanging from your ears, that's distracting, not chic. If jewelry is too anything--too big and flashy, too delicate to be noticeable, too cheap looking to be a convincing imitation of real stones or real gold--then it's not enhancing your overall look.

Versatile jewelry pieces have the potential to be brilliant or just plain bland, depending on the design. Opt for brilliant by choosing jewelry that takes an interesting twist on a classic piece. That piece of jewelry looks familiar, but there is some design element, such as texture or shape, that sets it apart from pieces that are more forgettable than fabulous. Medium-size hoop earrings consisting of band with an intricately sculpted design are more interesting than a plain hoop. A simple bangle bracelet that is slightly square is less predictable than the classic circle, but not weird enough to be considered a fashion fad.

One type of jewelry I wish the fashion police would confiscate and destroy is plastic beaded jewelry in bright colors. Since those pieces don't resemble any stone found in nature, they always look like cheap plastic. The one-dimensional colors of the beads make them hard to coordinate with clothes. If the beads are one shade of red and the clothes are a slightly different shade of red it looks off, or, to be painfully blunt, awful. Glass or natural stone beads reveal subtle color variations that are more versatile and attractive.

Even if the jewelry doesn't match the colors in an outfit exactly, it can still complement the colors of your outfit beautifully. If your closet has a serious case of the blues, jewelry that features inlaid abalone shell with all its different shades of blue, teal, and black make a lovely accent to all your blue clothes. Opals are another versatile option. These iridescent stones contain a virtual rainbow of colors and tend to mirror the colors around them. The way colors in opals dance in the light is simply stunning.

Instead of wearing one watch with every outfit, why not treat your timepiece like a piece of jewelry and invest in a bracelet-style watch or two? Stylish bracelet watches aren't always cheap, but it's sometimes a better deal to invest in one good quality bracelet watch than to buy one cheap watch for function and add a cheap costume bracelet on top of that for style. For a bolder statement, try a bracelet watch with wide links or a cuff bracelet with a watch face embedded in it. An up-to-the-minute watch charm attached to a link bracelet adorned with your favorite charms is a timeless way to show off your style.

Customize Your Necklaces

Sometimes the "wrong" piece of jewelry is really a diamond in the rough that just needs minor alterations to make it the perfect piece for you. I once found a delightful silver charm bracelet adorned with shoe charms. I was not delighted however, when I noticed the charms flopped around like a fish on dry land every time I moved my wrist. Instead of returning the costume bracelet I decided to convert it into a necklace. I bought another identical charm bracelet.

With needle-nose pliers, I removed the clasp from one end of each bracelet. On one of the bracelet end links with no clasp, I pried open the link and inserted the end link from the other bracelet that also had no clasp, and then squeezed the pliers around the open link to close it. Because I left a different clasp part on one end of each bracelet, the two bracelets linked together now form one necklace with a functional clasp. If taking apart your jewelry sounds scary, have a jewelry repair place make alterations for you.

Mixing and matching different pieces is an easy way to customize your jewelry. When I bought a necklace on clearance that featured a bold circular pendant featuring abalone shell infused with rich colors of teal, blue, and threads of black, I knew I would have to replace its disproportionately skinny chain. I kept my eyes open for a thicker chain to complement the pendant and eventually bought a necklace at Target with a chain composed of several strands of tiny black beads. Now I have the necklace I really wanted. The new chain has enough presence to complement the abalone pendant, and the touches of black in the abalone pendant coordinate with the black beads perfectly.

Necklace length can be tricky. The necklace that was the perfect length when worn against your skin suddenly comes up short when layered over a shirt with a collar. To add length to a necklace, find a link bracelet similar in color and style to the necklace. Simply unclasp the necklace and attach the bracelet to the necklace using the bracelet clasps. This should give you an extra six inches or more in necklace length. If that's too long you can always have some links removed from the bracelet, assuming you don't wear the bracelet and only use it as a necklace extender. Ideally, the coordinating bracelet will look as though it was part of the necklace all along. You may be surprised at how minor jewelry alterations can make a big impact on your look.

Chic Cocktail Rings

For an unapologetically glamorous piece of jewelry it's hard to beat a cocktail ring. Even the name sounds glamorous, subtly implying your evening plans include wrapping your bejeweled hand around a cool cocktail glass while engaging in lively conversations at some fabulous party. To further the illusion that you live a life of luxury, treat yourself to a nice manicure. Chipped nail polish or, even worse, dirty nails, will make even the most dazzling diamond look cheap. Well-groomed nails that are reasonably short and gently rounded at the edges look modern and sophisticated.

There are so many reasonably priced costume cocktail rings on the market that look convincingly like the real thing that there is no reason to wear a ring that looks like it came out of a gumball machine. A convincing cocktail ring stone mimics the facets, clarity, and sparkle of more expensive gems, and it is realistic in scale. A stone so big it looks as though it requires heavy lifting looks fake, even if it happens to be real.

The perfect cocktail ring complements the size and shape of your hand. Delicate fingers that would be overwhelmed by huge statement pieces can easily carry off more scaled-down versions with small to medium stones about the size of a pea. Hands with long fingers can get away with wide ring bands that visually shorten the fingers, while hands with shorter fingers may find narrower bands more flattering. A ring band with an open design that allows some of the skin underneath to show through doesn't visually shorten the finger the way a solid band does and is universally flattering.

To elongate the look of fingers, try an oval or rectangular stone that sits parallel to the finger. As for color, the stones of the ring can either relate to the outfit by mirroring the colors or the intensity of the colors in the outfit, or provide a pop of color to an otherwise subdued outfit.

The best way to showcase a cocktail ring is to give it as little competition as possible. Other rings on the same hand tend to distract more from the cocktail ring than complement it. One dramatic cocktail ring is plenty of adornment for one hand. For an impressive selection of glamorous jewelry, check out the appropriately named evesaddiction.com. Between the reasonable prices and the designer knockoffs, this jewelry retailer really is addictive.

A Common Scents Guide to Perfume

If your immediate destination includes a department store full of perfumes that entice you with their beautiful bottles and equally attractive scents, then don't bother applying perfume at home. Applying a scented product like perfume or body lotion before shopping makes it hard to distinguish new scents from the one you are wearing.

Instead of showering customers with perfume as they used to, perfume salespeople often hand shoppers a piece of paper with perfume sprayed on it. Ultimately a perfume smells different on paper than it does on the body, but this is still a good way to get a feel for the overall scent--floral, musky, fruity, etc. The perfume-scented paper saves you from having to apply several scents. It's best to limit yourself to a few scents when spraying them on yourself. Identifying one perfect scent out of the three sprayed on your arms is a heck of a lot easier than identifying that one perfect scent out of a dozen.

After you have sprayed perfume on your wrists, wait at least 20 minutes before deciding if you like the perfume. The scents may change slightly over time as they react to your body's chemistry. Do not rub your wrists together; this breaks down the perfume. After finding a scent that makes you swoon with pleasure, make a note of the name so you can buy it online for a cheaper price than you find at the department stores. My personal pick for price and selection is scentiments.com.

What are commonly called perfumes in the department stores are usually alcohol-based scents more accurately known as cologne. Real perfume is oil based and usually very expensive. To enjoy the rich, more complex scent of perfume in a sample size, go to luckyscent.com, where you can buy small vials of perfume. The samples are perfect for a special occasion when you want the more complex, longer lasting oil-based perfume but you don't want to go for broke buying the whole bottle.

Want to Make a Good Impression? Watch Your Mouth!

I was walking through an airport when I noticed another traveler. From afar she was a vision of polished professionalism. Her conservative suit was properly tailored, her coordinated shoes were stylish, and her hair and makeup spoke of a woman who understood the importance of proper grooming. What came out of her mouth however, spoke of a woman who doesn't have a clue. Her use of foul language was minimal, but her volume was not. I could hear her high, shrill voice from such a distance, it occurred to me that while I had admired her appearance from afar, her speaking voice made me want to get much farther away from her, like on another continent. Unless you are trying to warn others that the building is on fire, when you are indoors use your indoor voice!

Another time I was channel surfing on my TV when I was suddenly captivated by the image of a famous actress in a glamorous evening dress, accessorized by a bold gemstone necklace, expertly styled hair, and perfectly applied makeup. She looked stunning. Unfortunately the things coming out of her perfectly glossed mouth were also stunning. While acting as a presenter for a charity event, she used one R-rated swear word repeatedly throughout her presentation. After demonstrating her mastery of foul language, she went on to tell lame, tasteless jokes that generated a few halfhearted chuckles from a small portion of the audience. After that spectacle my lasting impression of her was that she has no class.

If you want to make a good impression, watch your mouth. No amount of fabulous clothing, makeup, and grooming will erase the negative impression created by low-class behavior. Talking in a way that respects the listener is one of the cheapest ways to make a positive impression, no fabulous evening dress required!

Shopping Smart is Always in Style

How to Dress for Shopping Success

There's a lot more to dressing for shopping success than carrying a handbag full of cash and coupons. A well-thought-out shopping outfit saves time in the dressing room and makes it easier to judge if potential purchases are flattering on you.

Wearing the right undergarments is crucial to judging the fit of a garment. When shopping for an evening dress for example, it's essential that you wear the same strapless, padded or plunging bra that you are going to wear with that evening dress. Not sure what kind of evening dress you are going to end up with? Try a convertible bra that allows you to arrange the bra straps in different ways or a bra with removable straps that can convert into a strapless bra if needed. If you intend to wear shapers to slim you down and smooth things over with your new outfit, be sure to bring a shaper with you or simply wear it while shopping.

One of the worst undergarments to wear while shopping for clothes is a sports bra that flattens your chest. Once you put on a regular, more uplifting, shapelier bra your bust looks as if it's ready to burst out of your new blouse. A regular bra that blends in with your skin tone, and nude-color, seamless panties are more flattering when trying clothes on.

What you wear shopping should never distract from the things you are shopping for. If you are shopping for a cute top, then wear bottoms in a neutral color. Trying on patterned or brightly colored tops with pants or skirts in a clashing color or pattern makes you look like a fashion victim, and it's harder to judge if the top is working or not.

Shopping for clothes generally involves a lot of dressing and undressing. It sounds fun and sexy, but the wrong clothes and accessories can make shopping a real hassle. Long necklaces that have to be removed every time you try on a top, bracelets too big to allow narrow-sleeve shirts to be tried on, big earrings that threaten to get caught in any garment you have to pull over your head, and rings or bracelets with prongs that snag everything in sight make trying on clothes a hassle. Try smaller earrings, avoid jewelry with prongs, and wear shorter necklaces. To make a dramatic statement with accessories, adorn yourself with stylish shoes, handbags, and a bold watch.

Shopping for clothes is often a race against the clock. At a women's clothing store I used to work for, it was common for panicked customers to practically fling themselves at the salespeople, explaining that they needed an evening dress for an event they were attending in two hours! Umm, good luck with that. Even if you're not in a hurry, the clothes you wear shopping should be easy to remove and put back on. A jacket that easily zips off or a cardigan worn over a lightweight fitted top like a tank top or lightweight T-shirt allows you to remove your outer layer easily and keep your tank or T-shirt on when trying garments with a more relaxed fit. Pants should be loose enough to remove easily, and slip-on shoes are a real time saver.

It's hard to visualize how an outfit will look when you are wearing the wrong socks. I once encountered a delightful customer wearing white athletic socks while trying on a glamorous evening dress. When she saw her reflection in the store's three-way mirror, she joked that the socks didn't quite work with the outfit. The customer saw the humor in the situation, but serious shoppers should opt for nude-color thin socks that practically disappear when shopping for new clothes and shoes.

Dressing for shopping success goes beyond clothes. Wearing enough makeup to prevent unflattering fluorescent store lighting from making you look like a walking corpse is a good idea, but apply makeup with a light touch. Makeup can easily rub off on garments you have to pull over your head to try on. Antiperspirant can also rub off on clothes, leaving conspicuous white marks behind. A clear antiperspirant starts off invisible and stays that way, leaving no icky white smears.

There is no reason to apply perfume before a shopping trip when department stores offer a generous selection of appealing perfumes just waiting to be sampled. Perfume is the one thing you can try on that doesn't require a dressing room, so sample away!

A Cut Above

Designer brands that rely heavily on status and slick advertising to sell their products are facing challenging times. Today savvy shoppers are more interested in spotting quality than sporting a designer brand. Once you know what to look for, it's easy to spot the hallmarks of better quality clothing to ensure you get your money's worth no matter where you shop.

Look for symmetry. Hold the garment out in front of you on the hanger. A bad hem is one that rises and falls like a roller coaster or looks uneven at the sides. When you set the handbag down on the counter, does it sit up straight or look crooked? Do the details, such as the length of the points on a collar, match on both sides? Are the patterns, such as plaids or stripes, perfectly lined up at the seams or do they look a bit off?

What is the item supposed to feel like? A high-quality handbag shouldn't feel like cheap vinyl. Any fabric that feels like sandpaper should be skipped, period. At normal room temperature, natural stones, like the ones found in jewelry, are usually cool to the touch. If a stone hasn't been sitting next to a hot display light or been on your body long enough to warm up and it doesn't feel cool, it might not be real.

Learn how to recognize better quality by doing a little hands-on shopping. Touch and examine the construction of better quality merchandise at a higher-end store near you. Focus on expensive, timeless pieces that rely more on their quality than a trendy image to attract customers. If you fall in love with a certain piece out of your price range, wait for a sale or look it up online to see if you can get a better deal.

See the light. Examine the fabric in garments by holding the piece up in front of you in the direction of a bright light in the store. Does the light showing through the single layer of fabric reveal areas of the material that are thin and uneven? Is there so much light showing through the fabric that you would have to layer the item over something else to prevent it from being too revealing? Are other shoppers giving you strange looks? Ignore them; you are on a mission to seek out quality, and trivial matters like public opinion don't concern you right now.

Stitching says a lot about a garment. Irregular, uneven stitching or loose threads look cheap no matter what you pay.

Keep an eye out for the kind of consistent, even stitching that makes the garment or handbag look like an investment piece, even if you invested very little in it. If there is more than one garment piece in your size and color, you can scrutinize them against each other and look for flaws to see if one is superior in overall quality, if only slightly. Ultimately one good-quality piece will do far more for your wardrobe than a dozen poor-quality ones.

Shopping Outside of Your Department

Ever since the slip dress slipped out of the lingerie department and onto the fashion catwalks, stylish women have been taking advantage of unexpected sources for both casual and dressy looks. It's now possible to find slip dresses and simple chemises in the lingerie department that would make lovely day dresses worth showing off in public. Of course they do need to provide decent coverage and not make you look like you just rolled out of bed. On the other hand, some skimpy, lightweight summer dresses are just as appropriate for the bedroom as the beach and make wonderful nightgowns.

Self-proclaimed stylists who declare dressing like a pop star half your age makes you look older, not younger, cause many women to avoid the juniors department for fear of looking silly. What these style experts are overlooking is that there are some very grown-up styles in the juniors department. Attractive T-shirts and sweaters, affordable accessories, and basic bottoms with a stylish twist often share retail floor space in the juniors department alongside the super-trendy items that are clearly a fashion don't for any woman past prom age.

Wandering into the men's or boys' departments increases your wardrobe options while potentially decreasing your cost. When I needed a pair of simple black sneakers at a reasonable price I looked at women's shoes from various retailers and found basic styles with big price tags. I was buying sneakers to run errands, not run a marathon, so why buy overpriced shoes? Eventually I strolled over to the boys' shoe section, where I found a pair of basic black sneakers cheaper than anything I found in the women's department. Of course boys' and men's shoes are sized differently from women's, so try on a few sizes to figure out which works for you.

The men's department is a great source for basics. For sweatpants that don't have words emblazoned across the behind, or a relaxed fit T-shirt that doesn't fit like a second skin, the boys' and men's departments are full of no-nonsense basics at no-nonsense prices.

After stocking up on basics in the men's department, check out the more stylish accessories there. A man's watch makes a bolder statement than a traditional woman's watch. When women's summer hats take on such epic proportions that they provide more shade than a beach umbrella, the less conspicuous offerings in the men's department are worth checking out. The brims on men's fedora or Panama-style summer hats aren't nearly as wide as many women's oversized sun hats. When the weather turns cold, head to the men's department for wool newsboy caps or other stylish headgear.

By shopping outside the places and departments you traditionally shop for certain items, it's easy to create a look that's as original as you are. When people compliment you on your stylish find, you can respond with "You will never guess where I found it!"

Cheap is Chic When You Shop Consignment Stores

For years consignment stores have been the secret weapon of chic women who possess more style than cash. Upscale consignment stores offer incredible deals on designer duds, often charging less than half the original price. Naturally, consignment stores located in more affluent areas tend to sell the better designer brands, so begin your shopping safari there before hitting other stores.

Like a thrift store, a clothing consignment store sells slightly used clothing. Unlike a thrift store, women's consignment stores often have extremely high standards for the merchandise they sell. Certain consignment store owners are almost as snobby as pricey, upscale stores selling only designer brands, which is why smart shoppers flock to them.

Save yourself the embarrassment of walking around in damaged designer duds by looking the merchandise over closely for stains, snags, or any other flaws before you buy. People may not recognize the designer brand you wear, but they will recognize the ugly gravy stain on the front of that light-color blouse as a food stain.

If you find something you like, buy it today because it may be gone tomorrow. The odds of the consignment store getting another one in the exact same style and size as the one that sold are about as good as your chances of winning the lottery.

Just in case the consignment store has an "all sales final" policy, try the garment on at the store to be sure it fits. If a high-quality piece requires minor alterations such as hemming or taking it in, it may still be a good deal. The narrow seam allowances in many garments are skinnier than a supermodel, which means the garment can't be let out at all. Skip the too-tight garments and keep looking for garments that fit properly or can easily be altered to fit properly. Just to be on the safe side, ask the cashier about the return policy before walking out of the store with your fabulous new find.

Do a little detective work and find out what the consignment store's schedule is for accepting and putting out merchandise. For example, if that consignment store stopped accepting winter merchandise from sellers two weeks ago, then you know not to waste time coming back next week looking for a fresh selection of winter clothes. If the store puts out new merchandise on Wednesdays, then that's the day to get first dibs on fresh offerings. Better consignment stores receive merchandise so frequently that you never know what you are going to find, which makes shopping even more fun. It's the thrill of discovering unexpected gems that transforms mere shopping into stylish entertainment.

Wardrobe Essentials are a Stylish Investment

How to Go Glam without Going Broke

Even if your social calendar includes more backyard barbeques than fancy balls, it's a good idea to add some dressier, more glamorous pieces to your wardrobe mix. I'm not talking about a wardrobe packed with fancy frocks. I'm talking about brilliant trend-proof pieces that rise to the occasion, whether it's a holiday party, a wedding, or some other elegant affair.

For occasions that are dressy but not formal enough to break out the tiaras and ball gowns, wear coordinating separates instead of a dress. Only parts of the outfit need to be dressy to create a dressed-up look. A knee-length skirt in dressy fabric like heavy satin elevates a basic sweater and skirt outfit into something special. A slim pencil skirt topped with a sweater embellished with fancy embroidery or beading at the neckline looks pretty and polished. The eye-catching embellishment eliminates the need for fancy accessories. You could simply wear pearl studs or diamond solitaire earrings and still look dressed up. A clutch purse in patent leather or metallic material is a terrific day-into-evening accessory that's just as dressy but far more versatile than a fancy evening bag.

Now let's talk about dresses. I believe this is the part where I am supposed to praise the little black dress for its versatility. I'm all for versatility, but I've worked in retail selling women's clothing, and I still remember the disappointed look women gave me when I suggested a tasteful little black dress. These women weren't looking for a dress so basic and forgettable that its personality could be completely transformed through the use of accessories. They were looking for a more exciting dress with real personality. After all, dressing up is supposed to be fun!

A distinctive dress can be worn repeatedly and still look fresh. If you are mingling with different groups of people on different occasions, then your audience has no idea that you have worn that stunning red dress before. Just avoid too much exposure. When you see the pictures of yourself at weddings, bridal showers, business networking events, and every other dressy occasion wearing the same dress, it starts to look as if you are in uniform, not in style. To make a dress look like a completely new outfit, layer a nice sweater or chic button-up jacket over the dress. Layering gives the illusion that you are wearing a top and skirt instead of a dress.

Plenty of luxurious-looking fabrics are created out of budget-friendly materials like polyester and cotton. The only fabric to avoid completely is acetate. Acetate is a weak, poor-quality fiber used for garments like prom dresses that are designed to be worn one time. A social butterfly like you demands more out of her party clothes than just one wearing!

Making Your Wardrobe Work

For us frugal fashionistas, the reality is that no matter how style savvy we are, there are pieces lurking in the closet and jewelry box that work pretty well but aren't fabulous enough to be considered "perfect." Learning how to make those less than fabulous pieces work for you is cheaper and easier than scouring stores for hours looking for those perfect pieces to add to your wardrobe.

Color and patterns are tricky. When colors are too subtle, they make you look washed out. If the colors and patterns are too bold for your figure and natural coloring, the clothes overwhelm you. The key to wearing a color or pattern that is too soft or loud is to pair it with its opposite. A pastel pink shirt that would look more at home in a retirement home than a fashion runway turns chic when paired with a cardigan or jacket in a rich raspberry. The richness of the raspberry compensates for the subtlety of the pastel pink.

The same strategy works for bold patterns. A blouse or dress in a larger-than-life print can be toned down a bit by layering a neutral-color cardigan or jacket over it. In spite of the fact that horizontal stripes make any woman not built like a supermodel look shorter and wider, women keep stocking their closets with stripes. Stand tall and show off your striped tops by layering them under a solid cardigan or jacket that tapers at the waist. The contrast breaks up the horizontal pattern. Another way to break up horizontal stripes on top is to wear a scarf or chunky necklace that drapes down the front of top. This strategy creates a strong vertical line that visually slices through the horizontal lines.

One of the frumpiest fashions to hit the fashion scene in recent years is the grandpa sweater. This unflattering long, shapeless cardigan proves that perhaps grandpa's closet isn't the best source for style inspiration. To make shapeless garments look less frumpy, pair them with streamlined fitted pieces. A long cardigan worn over a dark fitted top and tailored trousers, slim jeans, or a pencil skirt makes you look longer and leaner. To add some definition to a shapeless cardigan or dress, cinch the waist with a narrow belt and add discreet shoulder pads to help the sweater drape in a more flattering way.

Sometimes clothing comes up short, literally. Full-length shirt sleeves that are slightly too short can be rolled up for a more casual effect, and no one will suspect that your sleeves were too short to begin with. To make the shortness of the sleeves look deliberate, pile on the baubles and bangles. Adorning your wrists with layers of bangles on one hand and a boldly designed watch on the other will give the appearance that the shirt, with its slightly short sleeves, was designed to showcase your jewelry.

Basically, the secret to making less-than-perfect pieces work is to create an outfit that looks deliberate--as if you intentionally chose that frumpy fashion "don't" of a long cardigan sweater because you knew it would provide an unexpected twist to your sexy jeans and vintage rock-concert T-shirt ensemble.

Clothes That Go the Distance

After hearing from various fashion experts that a classic cashmere sweater was a "must have" investment that would look chic for years to come, I finally gave in and bought a black cashmere turtleneck--on sale, of course. This timeless piece that was supposed to last forever lasted exactly one season before I got rid of it. The sweater was unbearably hot when worn indoors. Sure, I like to wear clothes that are slimming, but sweating the pounds off was not what I had in mind!

Ever since that cashmere catastrophe I have ignored the fashion experts and created my own criteria for what's worth adding to my closet. One criterion for buying wardrobe basics is that the pieces must be able to make the transition from one season to another. I look for medium to lightweight tops, like simple knit shirts and sweaters (no cashmere) that can be layered over or under something else. And when the weather turns frosty, I simply layer my medium-weight pants over a pair of thin leggings.

Pieces that lend themselves to layering also create more stylish possibilities. A classic tailored vest in soft gray worn over a simple black T-shirt, black knee-length shorts, and a pair of stylish wedges is chic and simple. The same vest worn with a crisp blouse, tailored trousers in a traditional menswear fabric, and patent penny loafers makes a completely different style statement. For a sexier take on vest dressing, try wearing the vest over a strapless dress. The menswear-inspired vest is one example of a solid investment piece that enjoys the fashion spotlight now and then yet never quite seems to go out of style.

A key question to consider when buying something new is, how long is this item going to look fabulous? I refuse to buy certain styles of artsy woven tops because I look at the construction of their loosely woven ribbons or yarn as a major snag just waiting to happen. Garments with glued-on beads that look like they might fall off if I sneeze too hard are also a fashion no-no.

I will happily stock my wardrobe with basic black pieces, as long as those pieces are not made out of 100 percent cotton. I have an old cotton T-shirt that started out as deep rich black but eventually faded to a dark gray. Sure, I could dye it back to its original shade, but it's a basic T-shirt, for heavens sake. The cost of a bottle of fabric dye is probably more than a new T-shirt. For my basic black pieces I prefer synthetic blends that won't fade as fast, such as polyester blended with a breathable fiber like rayon.

The Summertime Hall of Shame

Summertime fashion articles are packed with advice about what to wear. The most flattering swimsuit for your figure, cute summer dresses, shorts in every shape and style, and sandals galore. Having done my fair share of shameless people watching during the warmer months, I have decided that what is really needed is advice on what *not* to wear for summer. Here is my summertime fashion hall of shame:

- Those chunky black strap sandals. Notice I said *strap*, as in one strap. One very wide black strap that acts as a big horizontal band attached to a flat chunk of a heel that visually shortens the foot while strangely looking out of season and more appropriate for cold weather due to its overall heavy appearance. Want to lose a few pounds for summer? Get lighter shoes!
- Visible bra straps with tank tops or anything else. It's called underwear for a reason. It's supposed to go *under* clothing. There is no excuse for lingerie abuse.
- A fashion faux pas most likely induced by heat stroke is the layered tank top look. I get how layering adds interest and color to an outfit. What I don't get is what makes women say to themselves, "It's 109 degrees out. I know! I'll add a layer of clothing!"
- Cheap plastic flip-flops. This fashion flop is cheap chic, without the chic. You can find nice sandals made of materials that look like linen, leather, or some other material actually derived from nature, not a laboratory. These sandals

have the same basic design as the flip-flop without giving off the whole "I don't spend more than $5 on summer shoes" vibe.

- Stand-alone swimsuits that don't relate to other articles of clothing being worn at all. The swimsuit says *tropical* with its exotic ethnic print. The shoes with their stripes and sports company logo say *100 percent sporty*. The oversize beach bag with its bright colored print says *I'm fun and whimsical and I can double for carry-on luggage in a pinch*. The oversize shirt says *I'm too cheap to buy a real swimsuit cover-up*. A swimsuit is part of a complete outfit. You wouldn't wear sneakers with an evening dress, would you?
- Weird-size sunglasses. As a general rule sunglasses should be larger than a pair of contact lenses and smaller than a beach blanket. Sunglasses are designed to protect the eyes, not shield the entire body.

I could give even more examples, such as feet not ready for public viewing in desperate need of a pedicure, etc., but the point is, casual is not the same as careless. Ballet flats with city shorts are one example of dressing casual and chic. Summertime is not the time to let your sense of style take a vacation.

Hosiery Helper

Once women discovered they could create the illusion of even skin tone through body makeup or bronzer instead of disposable panty hose that ran five minutes after you put them on, there was no going back. Sheer hosiery may have lost its appeal, but opaque tights are a fashion staple with a popular following.

Unlike sheer hose, opaque tights are very forgiving. They conceal everything from slight blemishes to the fact that you haven't gotten around to shaving your legs for weeks. A dark pair of tights looks slimming, but wearing black opaque tights with a black shirt can actually make your outfit look mismatched. That's because, strange as it sounds, there are different shades of black. The tights may be black with subtle gray undertones while the skirt may be a shade of black with brown tones. When wearing a black skirt, chocolate brown, burgundy, or charcoal gray tights are attractive alternatives to black. Textured and brightly colored tights only look good in a fashion shoot on tall, skinny models with nonexistent thighs.

Tights don't run as easily as sheer hose, but they will run faster that an Olympic track star if you're not careful. Before putting on a pair of tights, take off any of jewelry with prongs or sharp edges that might snag the tights. Now apply moisturizer to your legs to make the tights slide on more smoothly. Once you have your tights on, apply a layer of moisturizer on top of the tights from your waist to a few inches above your knee. Doing that reduces static cling between the tights and your skirt. Now all you need to complete your ensemble is a stylish skirt or dress, fashionable boots, a few well-chosen accessories, and a whole lot of attitude!

A Fresh Coat

A small wardrobe of fabulous coats can brighten your mood even on the cloudiest days. In a colder climate your coat makes frequent appearances, so be bold, be stylish, and don't be afraid of color and pattern when it comes to your winter coats. Take advantage of the reluctance of other shoppers to buy a winter coat in teal or red plaid, and hold out for hot deals on your cold-weather gear. On the other hand, holding out for incredible deals on a great classic coat is a bit of a gamble. Flattering high-quality coats tend to disappear off the sales racks faster than a snowball in summer. Sometimes you have to adopt a strategy that doesn't involve clearance sales to ensure you get the coat you want at a better price.

Visiting a better department store and taking note of the brand and style you like so you can shop for a cheaper version online is one way to go. Another approach would be to get on the store's mailing list. Sometimes you have to sign up for a store credit card to get the really good deals and coupons. Stores often give you a percentage off your first purchase when you open up a new credit card, which could add up to a serious chunk of change when buying a decent coat. A word of warning: Opening up a new charge account only works to your advantage if you can pay the bill off in full and there aren't any fees attached to the card when you pay in full. A cheaper alternative to department store prices, if you don't mind the limited selection, is buying coats at a consignment store.

Being bold and stylish works when you are building a coat wardrobe for the sake of variety. If your budget only allows for one coat that has to work with everything and last several seasons, perhaps the pumpkin orange pea coat isn't the best choice. The most versatile coat styles are classic in cut, say a trench coat style; neutral in color, such as black, gray or brown; and just a little above or below the knee in length.

Versatile coat styles take you from season to season. A water-resistant medium-weight coat with a removable, insulated lining provides warmth when you need it. When the snow starts to melt you don't have to melt with it in your too-toasty coat. Just remove the lining and wear your classic coat as a raincoat. Some coats are warm and cozy, but they don't repel water very well. Look for a description on the coat's hang tag flatly stating whether the coat is water repellent before you buy it.

When buying a coat, wear the bulkiest sweater or tailored jacket that you would be wearing with the coat to check for fit. Put the coat on and hold your arms out in front of you as though you are grasping a beach ball to be sure you can move your arms freely while wearing the coat. Ignore customers who look at you as if you are nuts. Obviously they are amateurs at this whole coat-shopping thing.

Now that you have done all that hard work of zipping up the coat and holding an imaginary beach ball, sit down and take a break for a moment. How does the coat feel when you are sitting? Notice the length of the coat and the volume of the coat when you are seated. When you stand up you should be able to get out of a seated position without excess fabric interfering with your movement or shifting around in a way that forces you to rearrange your coat so you don't look as if you slept in it. If you can sit, stand, move your arms, and actually afford the garment, then congratulations, you have a winner!

Exercising Your Options

The irony of wearing unattractive, baggy clothes while exercising to create a more attractive figure probably doesn't occur to most women as they sweat their way through their heart-pumping exercise routines. No, when a woman is exercising, her mind is focusing on less fashionable things, like not passing out during a strenuous routine. Before you take another exercise class, here are a few lessons in no-sweat style:

The wrong shoe color can visually shorten the body by breaking up the line between the feet and legs. Bulky, blindingly bright white sneakers weighed down with straps and frivolous design details exaggerate the size of your feet. Sneakers in a more subdued color such as light gray or taupe, with a minimal design accents, create a more harmonious look by blending in with the whole outfit.

Baggy T-shirts with low, droopy armholes inhibit movement and your sense of style. I remember one yoga routine I attempted while wearing a baggy T-shirt. During one pose I had to stand and then bend over with my arms outstretched. This caused my baggy T-shirt to slide down and engulf my entire head. While I was struggling to avoid getting smothered by my baggy T-shirt, the instructor kept gently reminding everyone to remember to breathe. Remembering to breathe wasn't my problem; my problem was trying to breathe through my T-shirt! A T-shirt in a solid color that fits properly and skims the body past the waist is the most flattering and least potentially dangerous style for any figure.

It should be that last set of crunches making you sweat, not your clothes. Pants in heavyweight fabrics like fleece, velour, and terrycloth trap sweat and weigh you down. Yoga pants in a medium-weight fabric with straight or slightly flared legs balance the hips and make the legs look longer. When paired with a cute knit shirt or sweater, yoga pants make the transition from gym wear to chic and casual daywear more gracefully than bulky sweatpants.

For an Uplifting Experience, Buy the Right Bra

Wearing the right bra can make the most of whatever you wear over it, so it's worth it to invest in quality and only wear proper-fitting bras. The foundation of any bra wardrobe is the basic T-shirt bra. This bra is so smooth that it discreetly disappears under unforgiving fabrics like lightweight jersey. You can buy these bras in fun colors, but at least two of your T-shirt bras should be in a neutral color that blends in with your skin tone and disappears under lightweight tops. That way you always have a clean bra on hand to discreetly support your curves.

If there is one fashion don't that stands out as being unflattering to an alarming degree, it's the droopy boob syndrome. Breasts that sag due to lack of proper support affect your silhouette, giving you a dumpy appearance. A properly supportive bra gives the breasts a gentle lift and creates a longer line between the breasts and the waist, which draws the eye up and makes you look slightly taller. Another benefit of wearing a well-made, supportive bra is that clothing will drape in a more flattering way.

For those times when you want to feel sexy and a neutral T-shirt bra isn't going to do the trick, feel free to indulge in something lacy, frilly, or just plain scandalous. The trick to wearing bras with more surface texture and extra detail is to wear them under tops made of forgiving fabrics. A top in a slightly heavier material with some texture, like a cable-knit sweater, allows you to indulge in your love for luxurious lingerie more discreetly.

Make it Last: Wardrobe Care and Storage

Give Your Clothes Some Breathing Room

Whether you are strutting around in Bloomingdale's best or Wal-Mart bargains, you want your clothes to last. One way to make clothes last longer and look better longer is to give them a little breathing room. Bras, for example, have stretchy fibers in the fabric that help the bra keep its shape and support your womanly curves. These fibers are sensitive to heat, which is why you never put bras in the dryer. Continued exposure to body heat can also make stretchy fibers such as Lycra lose their elasticity. After a bra has been stretched across your body all day, it needs time to breathe and return to its original shape. By alternating bras and never wearing the same bra for two days running, you can keep your bras in shape a lot longer. Hanging a bra on a hanger in your closet after a day of wear allows moisture to evaporate--and it doesn't look as tacky as hanging lingerie from a convenient doorknob.

Shoes also need breathing room. Leaving shoes in an open area for several hours after they are worn gives moisture a chance to evaporate before the shoes are stored in a box or some other enclosed container. Wearing the same pair of shoes every day wears them out a lot faster, because they don't have a chance to recover and return to their original shape after the previous day's use. So when you think about it, building a fabulous shoe wardrobe is just being practical.

If washing stylish clothes were as much fun as wearing them, dry-cleaners would be constantly overrun with fun-loving customers. Sometimes you can skip the hassle of cleaning hand-wash and dry-clean-only items by simply airing them out. If you wear the sweater or jacket layered over another piece of clothing, it doesn't come in contact with your natural body oils or beauty products like perfumes or hair spray, and it's not stained, then just hang it overnight on a dry shower rod or door handle to release any odors, such as cigarette smells, it may have absorbed. Giving it plenty of time to air out before putting it in your closet prevents the garment from transferring odors to other pieces of clothing.

Friction in the dryer can cause premature fading and pilling. To avoid this, turn garments inside out before tossing them in the dryer, and remove them from the dryer before they are completely dry. Over-drying sets in wrinkles, which forces you to iron so you don't look like a total slob. As an expert on avoiding unnecessary housework, I can tell you that sometimes it's possible to skip ironing altogether by removing pieces from the dryer when they are slightly damp and letting them hang-dry. A few minutes spent gently tugging on and manipulating certain pieces, like knit tops, into hanging straight without wrinkling may save you from ironing. Sweaters should be laid flat on a drying rack with a mesh panel to air-dry.

The downside of being so conscientious about air-drying clothes is that there comes a time when you need to wear that garment you just washed now, not after a couple of hours of leisurely air-drying time. To eliminate the final traces of dampness, put the garment on a hanger and use a hand-held hair dryer to dry the piece. With the hair dryer on a cool setting, put one hand inside the garment to separate the front and back layers of fabric while pulling the garment toward you slightly. Slowly pass the dryer back and forth about six inches over the damp spots until the garment is dry enough to wear. Or until you realize that you are running so late for your engagement that maybe wearing slightly damp clothes isn't such a bad idea. They will air-dry eventually, right?

Laundry Strategies to Make Your Clothes Last Longer

Finding a bra that fits, flatters, and gives you a little lift is such a shopping achievement that once you found the perfect bra, you want it to last as long as possible. A cheap way to extend the life of your bras is to put them in a mesh lingerie bag before running them through the washing machine. The bag protects your bras from getting wrapped around other clothes and stretched out of shape. It also protects other garments by preventing bra hooks from snagging them.

Mesh lingerie bags are intended for lingerie, of course, but if you're tired of trying to solve the mystery of how socks disappear in the dryer, buy a lingerie bag just for socks. Just toss them in the dryer while they are still inside the lingerie bag you washed them in. Lingerie bags are usually made of synthetic materials that don't always respond well to high heat, so don't set your dryer on blazing hot if you are going to toss in a lingerie bag full of socks.

Lingerie isn't the only thing designed to feel fabulous to the touch. There is nothing like stepping out of a shower and into the gentle embrace of a nice fluffy towel. Unfortunately, with repeated washings, commercial fabric softeners can build up on towels, making them less absorbent. Pouring 1/4 cup white vinegar into the wash with the rinse cycle not only softens fabric just as well as a fabric softener, it can also help remove fabric softener buildup from clothes.

For an environmentally-friendly stain remover, pour 1 cup vinegar and 1/4 cup baking soda into the washer after the wash has started and water is present to distribute this natural stain remover throughout your dirty laundry. Instead of using bleach on white fabrics, try adding 1/2 cup 3 percent hydrogen peroxide to the wash in the bleach cup of your washer or directly to the tub after it has filled with water. Then add your clothing. Eco-friendly 3 percent hydrogen peroxide is composed of water and oxygen but, this powerful cleaning agent may damage certain fabrics, so test it on an inconspicuous part of the clothes before washing them. Look for hydrogen peroxide at drugstores and mass retailers.

Keep Your Clothes in Great Condition

Taking proper care of your clothes is great for your budget because clothes last longer, and it's excellent for your image as well. When your clothes look terrific, so do you. A few preventive measures will keep your clothes looking newer longer.

Lavender sachets tucked inside your closet will repel moths and other fabric-loving insects. When it comes to fabric, moths have expensive tastes. They prefer to dine on natural fibers, such as fine wools, cottons, and even cashmere. Some people don't care for the smell of lavender, but having clothes that smell slightly of lavender is certainly more chic than having them smell like mothballs.

Nothing gets clothes bent out of shape faster than the wrong hanger. A thin wire hanger is the worst possible thing to hang your clothes on. It causes bumps in the shoulders of the garment and distorts its shape. The second-worst are probably hangers that are flocked to keep garments in place. The flocking can start to wear off after a while. Ideally a hanger should be about half an inch wide, depending on the type of garment it is supporting. A fine knit that tends to mold to the shape of the hanger may call for a more generously padded hanger. If a garment is loose-knit, bulky, or for any reason tends to lose its shape easily, store it flat in a drawer.

The clothes hanging in your closet should have a little space between them. Overstuffing your closet crushes clothes and causes them to wrinkle. Personally, not having to iron has provided an excellent motivation for cleaning out my closet and streamlining my wardrobe.

Handbags often end up in the dustiest parts of your closet, the floor or a shelf. To prevent your trendy totes from turning into dust catchers, put each handbag inside an old pillowcase before storing it in your closet. To keep leather handbags or shoes looking shiny and new, polish them with vegetable or olive oil before storing them.

Before putting anything in your closet, be sure it really is ready to wear. Look for stains, loose hems and buttons, or any other issues that you don't want to discover when you are halfway out the door. Ultimately, everything in your closet is there to make you look good with very little effort.

Thinking Inside the Box

Professional wardrobe stylists practically gush over the benefits of photographing each pair of shoes you own and attaching a photo to each shoebox to quickly identify the shoes inside the box. Perhaps if I strutted around in expensive designer shoes instead of my bargain ballet flats I might be motivated to do this.

An easier way to store and identify shoes quickly are photo boxes. Regular photo boxes can be found at mass retailers such as Target and at hobby stores. Buy boxes in different colors and/or patterns to reflect the different types of shoes you wear. For example, store your comfortable walking shoes in a photo box in with a map design printed on it. Spring shoes could be stored in light-color boxes or boxes with floral prints. Different color boxes can indicate the season or the dressiness of the shoe. Black shoes can simply be stored in black photo boxes.

Save your Kodak moments for interesting people and places, not your old sneakers. Instead of putting photographs of shoes on boxes to identify what's inside, label each box by writing a short description of the shoes on the card that goes in the holder on the front of the photo box. Wrap shoes in plain tissue paper, free of colored dye that could rub off on shoes. Group similar-themed boxes--dressy or casual, spring or winter--together on your closet shelf.

Stack shoe boxes in a way that makes the most sense to you. If you wear heels less frequently, put the higher heels on the bottom, slightly lower heels in the middle row, and your flattest shoes on top. Create a system that allows you to find your shoes quickly without having to read all the labels. This is also a great way to clean out your closet. You may end up discarding unwanted shoes instead of buying boxes for them.

Organize Your Handbag

No matter how stylish it is, a handbag is more than mere arm candy. A handbag should be both fabulous and functional, keeping things organized and easily accessible. And it should be the right size! Huge bags packed with so much stuff they weigh more than the woman carrying them, and overstuffed small bags straining at the seams are more fashion victim than fashionista.

Some women try to lighten their load by buying a smaller bag than the one they normally carry. This new bag often ends up being too small for their good intentions. Soon this bag is bursting at the seams with all the stuff that was in the old bag. The overstuffing distorts the shape of the bag which detracts from the stylish look of the bag.

If you want to lighten your load by making the switch to a smaller handbag, edit the contents of your purse before making the switch. First take everything out of your purse, piece by piece. Throw out expired coupons and receipts, pens that don't work anymore, lint-covered cough drops--anything you can't imagine needing or using in the immediate future. Items like Band-Aids and safety pins may be essential, but please limit the number of each "necessity" you carry.

Group related items together: a pen, small notepad for shopping lists, and coupons go together in a pocket. Pack only the cosmetic items you actually use when you are out. The cosmetics you decide to keep in your handbag go in a brightly colored cosmetic bag that's easy to spot. Have enough change on hand for an emergency phone call and an emergency candy bar (a snack attack does count as an emergency), but start a tip jar for the excess spare change that weighs your purse down.

>>>>>>>>>>>>>>>>>>>>><<<<<<<<<<<<<<<<<<<<<

Recommended Reading

How Not to Look Fat, by Danica Lo, offers the kind of realistic advice you could only get from a former plus-size model, not a size 2 fashion editor. Often irreverent, Lo's book on dressing slim covers a broad range of topics, including choosing flattering necklines, using scarves for stylish camouflage, and flattering haircuts for full-figured women. She also discusses such cheap tricks as the slimming effects of good posture and how to pose for a picture like a model.

Fashion for Dummies, by Jill Martin and Pierre A. Lehu is so full of useful information that if you don't collect fashion books the way I do, just buy this book and feel free to ignore other books that cover the fundamentals of fashion and style.

Fashion for Dummies is organized in a way that makes it easy to skip around and quickly find the topics that interest you. This comprehensive book covers everything from personal style, spotting quality, how to wear colors and prints in a flattering way, wardrobe building, and how to dress for special occasions. Helpful illustrations throughout the book show you what works and what doesn't. At over 300 pages long, *Fashion for Dummies* is a smart investment for any woman interested in looking her best.

>>>>>>>>>>>>>>>>>>>>><<<<<<<<<<<<<<<<<<<<<

Part Three: Beauty

"It's practical to look your best and be ready to take on the world."

--Estee Lauder

Cosmetics: How to Look Pretty While Pinching Pennies

The First Step in Buying Beauty Products is to Get a Second Opinion

Advertisements for cosmetics filled with seductive sales copy spouting the benefits of exclusive formulas and (allegedly) superior ingredients say a lot, but they don't answer the most important question of all: Does the product work? If you wonder whether that new lipstick is a smart buy or if you would be kissing your money good-bye for an underperforming product, go online and get a second opinion before you spend.

Total Beauty (totalbeauty.com) has many beauty-related articles, but its most useful feature is the product review section, featuring reviews by beauty addicts like you and me. Anyone can rate products and briefly explain why she loved or loathed that particular product.

If you are willing to spend a little money to find out which beauty products are worth the money, consider signing up for a membership to Beautypedia at beautypedia.com. Beautypedia is the brainchild of consumer advocate Paula Begoun, who has earned the nickname of Cosmetics Cop for good reason. The expert product reviews on her Web site completely ignore all the hype surrounding cosmetics and beauty products and are based on actual research on product ingredients and performance. The brutally honest beauty product reviews are unlike anything you would find in any advertiser-friendly fashion magazine.

Putting Your Best Face Forward for Less

Where you shop for budget-friendly cosmetic brands such as Revlon and Cover Girl depends on what kind of shopper you are. If shopping online is more appealing to you than standing in line at your local store, check out drugstore.com. The prices at drugstore.com are consistent with the kinds of prices you would find in a typical drugstore, but the selection is huge and the variety goes far beyond what you would find locally. If you are more of a strategic shopper, stocking up on beauty products when they go on sale or when you have a coupon, the ULTA store or its online presence at ulta.com are worth a closer look.

When you need that new eye shadow *now* and you simply can't wait for it to go on sale, Target and Wal-Mart are excellent choices for everyday low prices. Drugstores such as Walgreens have a respectable selection, but wait for a sale if you want to pay less than you would at Wal-Mart. Sometimes the regular Wal-Mart prices will be cheaper than the sale prices of another store, so don't assume you are getting the best deal because something is on sale elsewhere.

I never buy makeup at dollar stores. They tend to carry cosmetics from brands that I haven't heard of and brands that have gone out of business. A mass retailer like Target demands a high turnover of product and will put stuff on clearance to prevent old products from lingering too long. Constantly buying new products from cosmetic suppliers ensures that the products are not so old they have expired and become useless. Dollar stores, however, buy overstock and discontinued items, so it's possible that the products were out of date before they even reached the store. I don't care how cheap dollar stores are, wearing bad makeup ain't pretty!

Breaking Out of a Beauty Rut

If your beauty routine has become so routine you could practically perform it in your sleep, it's time to wake up to all the beautiful possibilities and try something new. While you are in front of your mirror, why not take a moment to add a little something extra to your beauty routine for a more finished look? Frame and flatter your face with well-groomed eyebrows. It only takes a minute to pluck stray eyebrow hairs to give your bushy brows a more polished look or to fill in sparse brows with an eyebrow pencil to give them more definition.

Whether you are the type of woman who feels naked without makeup foundation or you would rather reveal your naked face than conceal it under a layer of foundation, you could benefit from altering your makeup routine once in a while. Subtly blending foundation over certain parts of the face, such as under the eyes, creates the illusion of more even skin tone without the mask-like effect of a face completely covered with foundation. Applying foundation to parts of the face, followed by a light dusting of face powder on top, is sometimes more natural looking than a face completely covered with foundation.

For those times when your skin looks dull even with foundation, bring it back to life by applying a natural looking (not showgirl sparkly) illuminating product to brighten your skin tone. Illuminating products go by a variety of names with variations on the word "illuminate" or "radiance." Illuminating products are similar to foundation, but they contain light-reflecting ingredients intended to give your skin a subtle glow. For an even more subtle glow, apply an illuminating product as a highlight, to the top of your cheekbones, for example, instead of all over the face. Experimenting with new colors of eye shadows, blush, and lipstick is an obvious way to freshen your look, but playing with different textures allows you to try something new while still wearing your most flattering colors. If you normally wear a sheer lip gloss, try a moisturizing lipstick in a similar shade for a bit more impact. If powder eye shadow is the only thing you have ever worn, try wearing a cream eye shadow instead. A light dusting of powder applied to the lid before applying the eye shadow helps cream eye shadow last longer. Sometimes switching textures is good from a seasonal point of view. Dry winter weather can suck moisture out of your skin like a vampire, so try switching from a powder blush to a cream blush during the colder months.

Your lips may be your "best" feature but they aren't your only feature! Instead of making the same feature a dramatic focal point all the time, try spotlighting another one. For years designer Paloma Picasso was so closely associated with a certain shade of red lipstick that it became her signature shade. It was only when I saw a rare photograph of her wearing a much more subtle shade of pink lipstick and dramatic eye makeup that I noticed what intense and attractive eyes she has. When there are so many different looks that may be attractive on you, why settle for just one?

Is Your Face Ready for Fall?

While you are updating your fall wardrobe with all of its rich colors and textures, don't forget that your cosmetics need to be updated with the season as well. Sheer pastel lip colors and overly bronzed skin look as odd during the cold seasons as a snow skier in a bikini.

The oil-absorbing foundation or moisturizer that served you so well in the sweltering summer might not work as well in the fall and winter. To compensate for the drier fall air, consider switching to a foundation with less emphasis on oil absorption. Wearing heavier cold-weather clothing may indicate that it's time to break open a bottle of slightly heavier foundation. The heavier foundation that would have slid down your face in sultry summer months could be the perfect choice for nice, even coverage during the colder months.

The color of your foundation for fall may be slightly lighter than your summer color. For some women, less exposure to the sun results in a lighter skin tone. If your skin tends to change from golden glow to ghostly white, you can warm things up a little by using any leftover bronzer with peach or pinkish undertones as blush.

Cosmetics don't have to match the colors of an outfit (who wants to wear teal lipstick?), but they should match the tone of an outfit. Heavier fabrics in rich colors are best complemented by cosmetics with a little more presence, to prevent the face from looking washed out. Lipsticks that are stronger in color and a little more opaque than the summer sheers are a great place to start. To dilute a lipstick that is coming on a little too strong, apply a sheer lip gloss, then apply a layer of the heavier lipstick on top of the gloss.

Add some drama to the eyes by wearing an eye shadow that's slightly darker than your regular eye shadow. If you normally wear a light champagne-color eye shadow, for example, consider a slightly darker shade in taupe with some gray undertones. Adding one extra layer of mascara to your lashes and using an eyebrow pencil are easy ways to create more captivating eyes. Now you are ready to put your best face forward during the cooler seasons.

Facing the Camera

Whether you are attending a family gathering, a photo-friendly business event, or partying it up, always be prepared for your close-up. Unless you have the photogenic features of a supermodel, the camera tends to magnify flaws. As a result, pictures end up looking more like your hideous driver's license photo than any Kodak moment. To improve your image, adopt a few photo-friendly strategies.

Having the time to do full-on glamour makeup and get every hair in place before social gatherings is about as realistic as Santa depositing a professional makeup artist at your door. Instead, look back on photos that have been taken in the past, looking for anything you would love to have airbrushed out of the picture. It may be dark circles under your eyes that make you look like a zombie, a red nose that comes from having a cold or just stepping in from the cold, or a minor bump or scar that's maximized by the camera. Whatever it is, take an extra minute or two to apply a discreet amount of foundation or concealer to the problem area. From there apply as much makeup as you feel comfortable wearing and have time to apply. A light dusting of powder across areas that tend to get oily helps you save face in front of flash cameras that reflect the slightest shine.

Are your lips camera-ready? It's pretty obvious when very dark or bright lipstick starts fading. The lipstick starts to disappear from the middle of the lips, making it look as if you applied lip liner and forgot about the lipstick. Either choose a lipstick that can outwear and outlast hours of drinking, eating, and shameless gossip, or try a shade close to your natural lip color that won't be so obvious when it fades.

After arriving at your destination and exchanging proper hellos with the host, make a beeline for the nearest bathroom to freshen up. This gives you a chance to touch up your makeup and brush your hair before the picture-taking begins. After all, the only thing worse than having a bad hair day is having it immortalized in pictures.

Lash Out: Make the Most of Your Eyelashes

Batting your eyelashes is either a flirtatious gesture or a sign that your mascara-drenched lower lashes are sticking to your top lashes. To avoid the risk that every man within 20 feet will mistake a case of bad mascara for intense flirting, get the right mascara for the job. Ask yourself what it is you need your mascara to do. If you are going swimming or subjecting yourself to a tearjerker situation like a wedding (the fact that the real reason you are crying is because you had to spend your own money on an ugly bridesmaid's dress will be our little secret), then a waterproof mascara is the obvious choice.

The two most common colors of mascara are brown/black and black. Brown/black is a deep brown that is more subtle than black. This is a good choice for fair-skinned divas on whom black mascara may look severe. Brown/black is also a good color choice for daytime mascara if you want to save the more dramatic eye makeup for evening.

A good quality drugstore mascara is a better investment than a pricier prestige mascara. No matter how cheap or expensive it is, mascara goes bad a few months after it is opened and must be replaced. I tend to avoid volumizing mascaras for fear of looking as if I have small furry animals attached to my eyelids. If I want thicker-looking lashes, I can simply add another coat of mascara, coating the top and bottom sides of my lashes, for example, instead of just the bottom.

Eyelash curlers open up the eye area and make the eyelashes more noticeable by curling lashes upward. Follow instructions that come with the eyelash curler and be sure to curl lashes before applying mascara so you don't leave mascara smudges on the curler.

Applying a thin line of dark liquid eyeliner at the base of the eyelid, where the lashes meet the eyelid, makes the lashes look longer. The dark line makes the ends of the lashes visually recede. To downplay the presence of eyeliner, apply a thin line of eyeliner and then apply foundation and eye shadow to the eyelids as you normally would.

Seeing Red

For many women the idea of reducing eye redness and puffiness by lying down and putting a slice of cucumber over each eye is impractical, time-consuming, and a waste of perfectly good produce. If red, bloodshot eyes are staring back at you when you look in the mirror, here are a few strategies to help you go from bloodshot to bright eyed in no time.

Before applying eye makeup, run a washcloth under cold water and wring out the excess water. Put the cold washcloth over your eyes for a minute or two. Grab your eye shadow brush and a bottle of Visine or some other brand of redness-relieving eye drops. Work a drop or two of the eye drops into your eye shadow brush before applying eye shadow. While the eye brush is still a little damp, apply eye shadow across your entire lid. The addition of eye drops to the eye shadow helps the color stay on longer and reduces redness on your eyelids.

Avoid any eye cosmetic that is reddish in tone. Pink or orange cosmetics with reddish undertones make eyes look more red and bloodshot. A thin line of cool dark blue eyeliner or navy mascara discreetly brightens the eye area so when people look into your eyes they won't be seeing red.

Brighten Your Smile

There is no cosmetic on the market that can enhance the face the way a genuine smile can. Fortunately, a dazzling smile is easy to achieve for just a few dollars. To whiten teeth, wet your toothbrush with water and sprinkle about half a teaspoon of baking soda into the palm of your hand. Dip the wet toothbrush into the baking soda, then brush your teeth. For noticeable results, do this at least once a day before brushing your teeth. This whitening treatment is not a substitute for brushing your teeth with regular toothpaste, but it's a great substitute for all the fancier, more expensive treatments on the market.

Drinking certain beverages, such as coffee or tea, can stain teeth and make them look dingy. To prevent dark drinks from staining teeth use a reusable straw. Make sipping more festive by using one of those reusable plastic silly straws that come in twisted shapes for cold drinks, or buy a stainless steel straw for hot or cold drinks.

If blue-based lipsticks with cooler undertones look good on you, you're in luck. Cooler shades of lipstick that aren't orange or yellowish in tone make teeth look whiter and brighter. Red lipsticks can be either cool or warm in tone depending on the shade. If cooler shades aren't flattering on you, you can still dazzle everyone with your bright smile and brilliant personality.

Shed Some Light on Your Beauty Routine

The ideal lighting for applying makeup is natural light that is bright enough to apply makeup but not bright enough to exaggerate every flaw. If your bathroom doesn't provide adequate natural lighting, consider using a mirror that is lighted on the sides. While overhead bathroom lighting creates shadows, a mirror with lights on the side provides balanced, even lighting without the shadows.

Some clever mirror manufacturers make lights with adjustable settings to simulate day, evening, home, or office lighting. This is a brilliant idea because makeup that looks understated for day can look washed-out at night. A word to the wise: if you have a chance to look at your skin in a magnified mirror, don't! Magnifying mirrors make your pores look like potholes and grossly exaggerate the slightest flaw to the point that you start to think what you really need is not a new shade of blush but a bag to put over your head.

Making the Most of Your Beauty Products

Attractive Solutions for Your Makeup Mistakes

Lurking in your cosmetics drawer are your deep, dark secrets. Like the bright red lipstick that was supposed to evoke the sophistication of Coco Chanel but really made you look more like Coco the Clown. Of course you don't want to keep expired cosmetics, but what do you do with all those makeup mistakes? My advice is to dig into your pile of cosmetics cast-offs and make those mistakes work for you.

Lipstick mistakes can easily be fixed by combining lipstick with other cosmetics. To tone down a shockingly bright shade of lipstick or lighten a dark shade, dilute the color by first applying sheer lip balm or gloss to lips and then apply the lipstick with a lip brush. Lip balm layered under a too-dry lipstick makes that lipstick feel creamier. Color opposites can work great together when blended properly. Brown lipstick worn under a bright pink lipstick dilutes the brightness of the pink shade, while the pink adds some pizzazz to the otherwise dull brown. Have fun and experiment with different combinations.

To avoid transferring old shades of lipstick to your lips, clean the lipstick brush by swirling it in shampoo in the palm of your hand, rinsing it out with water, and letting it air-dry every time you change lipstick shades completely.

Eye shadow colors that are coming on too strong can easily be toned down. For powder eye shadows, apply the shadow with a fluffy brush across the upper or lower lid. The fluffier brush will distribute the powder with a lighter touch than a regular eye shadow brush. Dark as night or extremely bright eye shadows are easier to wear when you use them as an eyeliner instead of applying them all over the eyelid. Use a small eyeliner brush to apply the eye shadow along the base of your eyelashes to line the eyes.

Foundation color should always blend in with your current skin color. Foundation applied during the winter on paler skin may look like a mask when the season changes and your skin gains a warm summer glow. A foundation that's a little too light can be dotted under the eyes and blended with your correct foundation color as if you were applying an under-eye concealer. Off-color foundation can also be used as an eye shadow base. Apply the foundation to the upper and lower lids, dust lightly with face powder that blends in with your skin color, then apply eye shadow as usual.

Bronzer is another beauty product that needs to look natural at all times. Even if the color is right, applying it all over the face means that your face may not match the rest of your body. Apply bronzer in new ways, perhaps as a subtle eye shadow. A bronzer with peach undertones lightly applied as a blush lends a healthy glow to skin.

Learning how to make your mistakes work for you instead of throwing out these cosmetic blunders allows you to have fun and experiment with makeup while still being frugal. I've had my share of cosmetic catastrophes, and making the most of my mistakes has proven to be far more satisfying than sticking to a color palette of safe, boring neutrals.

Double-Duty Cosmetic Primers

Cosmetic primers are liquid or creams designed to be applied under another layer of makeup. The idea behind primers is that they will provide a better surface for makeup to adhere to. Professional makeup artists sing the praises of these primers, but the response from women with limited time and money has been less than enthusiastic. Fortunately, there are plenty of cheap ways to prime your face for makeup without using a primer.

First, start with great skin. By doing the obvious, drinking plenty of water and eating healthy, you are feeding the skin what it needs to look its best. Follow some sort of regimen appropriate for your skin type that involves regular exfoliation to remove dead skin cells from the face and lips. This creates a smoother surface for foundation and lipstick. If your skin is dry, apply moisturizer under foundation. This allows your skin to draw moisture from the moisturizer so it doesn't have to draw moisture from the foundation, which can leave the foundation looking patchy.

Instead of eye shadow primer, use a light layer of foundation topped off with a light dusting of powder. Then apply your eye makeup as usual. The eye area is often a little oilier than the rest of the face, so avoid moisturizing foundations, which won't last as long. A light layer of foundation and powder on the lips, blotted with tissue, conceals the color of your lips. This lets the lipstick you wear reveal its true color and also makes your lipstick last longer. Another way to prime lips for lipstick is to apply lip balm under lipstick. Use these techniques, and your face will be ready for prime time in no time!

Eye Makeup Removers You Already Have

Fewer beauty products in your bathroom means more money in your wallet, so before buying another bottle of eye makeup remover, consider a few affordable alternatives. Skin moisturizing organic extra-virgin olive or coconut oil can be used in a pinch to remove eye makeup. If you prefer beauty products that don't come from the pantry, gentle face cleansers are safe to use for removing eye makeup. Read the instructions on the bottle to see if it can safely remove eye makeup. Allowing the eye makeup remover to sink in for a few minutes while you wash your face makes it easier to gently remove the eye makeup with less rubbing. The less rubbing of the delicate skin around the eye area, the better.

Save a Few Bucks with the Right Beauty Brush

The right cosmetics brush is not only a great tool for making you look fabulous, it's a great tool for saving money, too! Take lip brushes for example. Using a lip brush allows for a more precise application of lipstick than just swiping the lipstick tube across your lips. It also allows you access to the lipstick at the bottom of the tube that would be difficult to get at otherwise. With a lip brush, not a drop of your favorite lipstick goes to waste.

A foundation brush used for applying liquid or cream foundation is more precise than using your fingers and ultimately cheaper than using sponges. Disposable cosmetic sponges absorb foundation, resulting in the product running out faster. Because sponges are rarely washed and reused like a cosmetic brush, they have to be replaced regularly. A quality foundation brush has synthetic bristles that don't absorb the product, and it lasts a lot longer than a cosmetic sponge.

Beauty Kits Take the Guesswork Out of Skin Care

My highly unscientific approach to skin care had been to buy whatever budget-friendly beauty product happened to be on sale. I decided to change my haphazard approach by buying a skin care starter set with a 30-day supply of various skin care products--on sale of course.

Products in the same skin care line complement other products in the line. For example, if you buy an exfoliating cleanser from one brand and a moisturizer designed to renew the skin by removing dead skin cells from another brand, the result might be too much exfoliation. Instead of showing off a youthful glow, your rosy face would look like you forgot to use sun block.

Another benefit of buying a starter set is that it usually contains a 30-day supply of beauty products. This is enough time for the products to show results. I would rather buy a 30-day supply of something I might not like than a bottle with six months' worth of the product in it. After the 30 days I will have a much better idea of whether the products are worth buying in their full-size versions.

So the next time you are checking out a new beauty lotion, see if that skin care line has some sort of starter set. The price for a set of multiple smaller bottles of different products can be about the same as one full-size bottle of lotion. You might buy the set for the moisturizer and find out the cleanser is the real standout. That's the beauty of starter sets.

The Beauty of eBay

Having gotten great deals on eBay for everything from electronics to home decor, it eventually occurred to me that I should seek out great deals on beauty creams as well. Fantasies of snapping up expensive beauty creams at bargain-basement prices were shattered when I went online and realized thousands of other women had the same idea and were willing to pay close to the regular retail price for the items, sometimes more. Cheapness ultimately triumphed over my desire for the latest prestige brand miracle cream, and I bought a beauty cream from one of the bargain brands.

Buying samples of expensive creams is a great way to try a product before shelling out for a more expensive full-size jar. Samples should cost far less, since the seller probably got them free from the cosmetics supplier. As with any item, it's smart to read the description closely to find out what you are really buying. Some sellers show a photograph of a full-size jar when what they are really selling are samples. Always buy creams that are sold in their original, never-opened jars. When beauty cream is transferred from the original jar to another container, it can be exposed to bacteria that reduce the effectiveness of the cream and may be transferred to the person who ultimately uses the product.

Unless you really are interested in all 652 beauty products offered by a certain brand, you can narrow your options by typing in the brand name and one word that refers to the product you are looking for in the search box. Typing "Prestige Brand eye" brings up eye products only and not the entire range of beauty products offered by that brand. Different sellers use different words to describe their products, so typing an overly detailed description could eliminate some sellers who were offering the exact product you are looking for.

Getting a great deal is always a beautiful thing. The best way to tell if you are getting a good deal is to go to a price comparison Web site (type the words "price comparison" into an online search engine) and find out what the beauty item is selling for at other retail locations. Vanity is no excuse for being a sloppy shopper.

Bacteria Isn't Beautiful

Friendship is about sharing. You share so much with your friends, it seems only natural to want share beauty products with them. Don't do it! When your skin comes in contact with beauty products, the interaction introduces bacteria into the beauty product that can be transferred to the next person who comes in contact with it. It's possible to give someone an eye infection from shared mascara or transfer germs from a borrowed lipstick. Feel free to share your beauty tips with your friends, but please keep your germs to yourself!

If a friend expresses an interest in a certain beauty product I use I will tell her what it is and where to get it. If it's a fun product like a lip gloss or shimmering body cream, I make a mental note to include a brand-new, unopened package of it in her next birthday or Christmas gift.

The only products I would consider sharing are those that use a pump spray for delivery, so the product never comes in contact with skin until it has been released from its container. Sometimes being a good friend means not sharing.

Snipping Hair Care Expenses

The Kindest Cut

The only thing worse than getting a bad haircut is paying top dollar for that horrifying hairstyle. I always get my hair cut at a local beauty school. I do occasionally get less than stellar haircut, but at less than $10 for a cut, wash, and blow dry I can at least take comfort in the fact that I didn't break the bank to look bad.

Beauty schools are great for a lot of reasons besides their low price. Your hair is usually done by students who are so afraid of cutting too much off that they trim off a little at a time instead of carelessly whacking off more than you wanted. Because students are learning, they tend to ask a lot of questions and really pay attention to what they are doing. Haircuts are checked by a trained professional who polishes up anything the student may have overlooked.

You will probably have to pay cash for your cut, but you won't have to pay much. In the end you pay for a haircut what you would have paid in tips at a fancy salon. To find the best beauty schools in your area, visit beautyschoolsdirectory.com.

Take Hair from Bland to Beautiful

If fear of getting a bad haircut that makes you look like a fashion victim is preventing you from trying a new style, don't worry--there are other ways to freshen up your hairstyle. Instead of a drastic new haircut, try new colors and styles. Subtle highlights can brighten your look without making the change too obvious. To add depth to your hair color, consider asking your hair colorist about low lights. Low lights add dimension to your hair by deepening the color in certain areas.

A new hair color can be fabulous, but it can also be high maintenance if it's not close to your natural hair color. Instead of committing to a totally new color, you can subtly alter your own hair color with a hair glaze. A colored glaze adds a semitransparent layer of color to your hair that enhances the vibrancy of your natural hair color. Because the glaze doesn't replace your own hair color, roots are a lot less obvious when the glaze starts to fade. The hair glaze can be applied by a salon stylist, or you can choose an over-the-counter glaze available at drugstores and mass retailers as a more affordable alternative.

I must confess, I repeatedly go for what is probably the world's most boring haircut, a simple bob. I continue to get this cut because I like getting cheap haircuts from students at the local beauty school and this particular hair cut is pretty much impossible to screw up. One time I was fortunate enough to have a beauty school student with flair for hair who saw styling potential in my incredibly bland choice of haircut. With my blessing, she scrunched and sprayed the bottom portion of my hair to take full advantage of my hair's all-but-ignored slight natural curl. Instead of just hanging the way it normally did, my hair looked a bit wild and untamed in a "just rolled out of bed and onto the set of a fabulous fashion shoot" sort of way. I loved it.

The wonderful thing about people in the beauty business is that they are often able to see potential in you that you may have been completely unaware of. Instead of getting stuck in a beauty rut, try getting the occasional makeover or talk to a hairstylist who can give you fresh ideas in making the most of what you have.

Hair Color Helper

At some point even the best dye job is going to fade. Frequent washings and sun exposure can take your hair from rich brunette to just plain blah pretty fast. That's why I use colored hair glazes that can be applied at home to deposit a sheer layer of color on top of my own color. The effect is subtle, certainly not a substitute for a dye job, but the color does gradually build and become a bit more obvious with repeated use.

A color glaze can slightly darken brunettes, add some richness to reds, and keep blond tresses shiny. If you are dying your hair a lighter color than your natural hair color, keep in mind that color glazes will not lighten hair or make dark roots less noticeable.

My strategy is to start using color glazes shortly after dying my hair and stop using them a few days before I dye my hair again. This way I can shampoo away the buildup of glaze product so it does not prevent the permanent hair dye from absorbing properly.

Instead of applying a colored hair glaze in the shower, I like to apply it to dry hair right before I go to bed and leave the glaze in all night. In the morning I simply wash the colored hair glaze out with gentle shampoo. This technique allows the glaze to really sink into my hair and add more color. It also allows the glaze to add more color to my pillowcase, so I make a point of using cheap pillowcases that can stand up to frequent washings.

To avoid staining your pillowcase altogether, try tossing a cheap towel over your bed pillow.

Hair Color to Dye For

While colder weather brings a return to deeper colors like deep plum for the lips, eyes, and nails, even the most ardent beauty queen will often overlook the one place where an application of rich color has potential to dramatically improve her look--hair color. Dramatic eye and lip colors make dull, faded hair color even more obvious. Hair color can be given a boost by deepening hair color to a rich chocolate shade, adding a little spice with red undertones, or brightening up your blond.

For those of you concerned about potential hair-color horrors, like the time I dyed my hair too frequently and it turned a bright, scary pumpkin orange, try a nonpermanent color formula within a few shades of your natural color. I like Natural Instincts from Clairol for its budget-friendly price and the natural looking (no bright orange) results. This ammonia-free hair color adds a layer of color to hair that gradually washes out in about twenty-eight shampoos, so the color disappears in a gradual, less obvious way than permanent hair color. In other words, you won't have the skunk stripe thing going on where your hair is parted a few weeks after applying the color.

Before You Hit the Beach, Hit the Bottle

During warmer months wearing a hat protects hair color from fading in the sunlight, but you can't dive into your favorite swimming hole with a hat on. Well, you could dive in with a hat on, but I don't think it would do much for either your swimming technique or the hat.

Once you go from frolicking on the land to splashing like a mermaid, you have other hair issues to deal with besides the sun. Chlorine from pools and ocean salt water can cause serious damage to hair, including drying it out and, in the case of chlorine, possibly changing the color to a lovely algae green depending on your hair color.

Before taking a swim, take a few minutes to apply a lightweight conditioner to your hair. The conditioner acts as a barrier between your hair and those unfriendly waters, so be sure to saturate your hair completely and allow the conditioner to sink in before diving in.

There are more hair conditioners on the market than I can count. Some of them are specifically designed to protect your hair at the beach. Instead of slathering your hair with expensive conditioner that's just going to wash out to sea anyway, try a cheap all-natural hair conditioner like organic coconut oil. Olive oil is another terrific hair conditioner, but coconut oil smells more natural and exotic at the beach, where olive oil makes you smell like a salad dressing. Put a little coconut oil in a plastic travel bottle, and you have the perfect poolside hair-care product.

The Body Beautiful

Wake Me Up Before You Go-Go

A bracing cup of caffeine-fueled coffee in the morning may be a more effective eye-opener than your alarm, but coffee isn't the only way to wake up in the morning. Try some simple stretching exercises to get the blood flowing and the brain focused. They are also a healthy way to release some stress before facing a day that might make you wish you had stayed in bed.

Choose a body wash with a stimulating scent for your morning shower. Look for citrus scents or the word "energizing" on the label, and inhale deeply from the bottle before applying it. Finish off your shower on a refreshing note by adjusting the water temperature to a slightly cooler temperature for the last few minutes of your shower.

Play some pop music so upbeat it could be prescribed as an antidepressant. I recommend "Wake Me Up Before You Go-Go!" by Wham. It's perky almost to the point of annoying, and there is the serious risk that the song may be stuck in your head all day, but, hey, at least you're up.

Soak Up the Savings

There is nothing like a long, hot shower to wash the stress away. Unfortunately, it's not only your stress being washed down the drain; your cash is also disappearing with every gallon of water you use.

To save water while still coming clean, try replacing your showerhead with a specially designed water-saving low-flow or adjustable showerhead. Four 15-minute showers a week at the lower setting could potentially save more than 100 gallons of water a month, depending on the showerhead design. No matter what kind of showerhead you have, you should never spend more than 15 minutes taking a shower. All that water beating down on you for an extended period of time strips skin of its natural oils.

To save time and water, wash your face when you take a shower. Get in the shower and splash some water on your face while the water is still warming up. Now gently massage the facial cleanser into your skin. In the short time it takes to apply cleanser the shower should have warmed up. Now that the water is warm, you can rinse off your facial cleanser, then proceed to take your shower.

There are other ways your beauty routine can cut your water bill. Don't have water running while you are brushing your teeth. When you are ready to rinse out your mouth, then turn on the water. When you are ready to open your water bill at the end of the month, turn on a smile!

Save Cash with Coconut Oil

Sometimes it's the seemingly nutty natural beauty treatments that work the best for your body and your budget. Many health-conscious people believe that what you put on your skin may be absorbed into the body. As much as I would love to play it healthy and buy the yummy organic skin-care products that feature everything from fruits to sugar to chocolate, I'm afraid these exorbitantly priced products would leave me with great skin but a naked bank account.

For a cheap and effective alternative, skip the beauty aisle at the store and check out the health food aisles instead. Organic extra-virgin coconut oil makes a terrific moisturizer. While fancy body creams can easily cost more than $20 for less than 12 ounces, a jar of organic coconut oil often sells for less than $20 for 29 ounces.

Coconut oil is so rich you only have to use a little--anywhere from a teaspoon to a tablespoon-- to cover your entire body. It's hard for the skin to absorb a heavy layer of oil, so apply only a very thin layer of oil.

The downside of coconut oil is that it takes at least a few minutes to absorb, so you can't put your clothes on right away. Also, it is solid at room temperature, so you may have to spoon it out of the jar in order to apply it. The upside of this bargain beauty product is that after using it at night you can wake up with soft skin and more room in your beauty budget for the kind of pampering indulgences that don't come from the food aisle.

Keep Skin Soft During Dry Winters

Seasons change. One thing that might change about your beauty routine during the harsh, dry winter months is that you either start wearing moisturizer or change to a more intense moisturizer to keep your skin soft and supple. One thing that shouldn't change during the winter months is that you still wear some sort of sun protection on your face, since you still have some exposure to the sun. Whatever moisturizer you choose, remember that gently exfoliating the top layer of your dry winter skin on a regular basis, at least once a week, will allow any moisturizer to penetrate more easily.

The Great Face-Off

Nowadays it seems there is a lotion or potion for every part of the body. Eye creams, hand creams, foot creams … what's next? Ankle cream? Instead of stocking up on different creams, try using beauty products meant for the face that didn't work the way you wanted them to for other parts of your body. Products designed specifically for the delicate facial area should be gentle enough to use elsewhere.

When a depuffing eye cream I purchased turned out to be nothing more than a glorified heavy moisturizer, I applied it to my hands at night for soft, silkier hands while making a point of not buying the product again. I once bought an exfoliating face wash that was so effective I think it may have removed more than one layer of skin. After taking a look at my red face in the mirror, I decided to use this abrasive face wash in the shower on parts of my body with tougher skin, like my heels and elbows. I can now show off my sandal-ready feet instead of my tomato-red face.

A face sunscreen I once used started off fine, but after a while it would begin to melt and drip down into my eyes, irritating them. I used up the product by wearing it as a regular sunscreen on my body. So before throwing away that moisturizer that makes your face feel like it was dipped in grease, ask yourself, "Would this greasy cream soften my elbows?"

Stay Financially Fit with Your Local Community Center

Several months after joining a local gym I became unemployed. To save some money, I called my gym and attempted to get out of my long-term contract. The shockingly insensitive customer service person snapped, "Well, you are going to get another job, aren't you?" and refused to let me out of my contract. After that nasty incident I vowed never to join a gym or sign any long-term contracts that I couldn't get out of.

After giving up gyms I focused on walking and exercise DVDs for my exercise. The problem was that at home with just me and the TV I can end the workout the minute I get tired or bored or decide I'd rather exercise my brain and curl up with a good book. The one thing a structured exercise class provides that you can't get from any exercise DVD is peer pressure! To stay motivated through an entire exercise routine I needed the threat of serious embarrassment. The kind of embarrassment that comes from quitting in the middle of a class while some gray-haired lady wearing a "World's Greatest Grandma" T-shirt is still keeping pace with the instructor.

As an alternative to regular gyms with their high-pressure sales pitches and ironclad contracts, I take advantage of the exercise classes at my local community center. For an incredibly affordable price I can take one class with no commitment to ever take another. I also have the option of paying for one month of classes, or several months of classes. A monthly membership allows me the freedom to mix things up, take all kinds of classes, and quit any class I don't like. One day I can go all Zen and take a Tai Chi class, and the next day I can get into the groove and dance (badly) to Latin music or lift weights in a strength and conditioning class. The variety of classes is far superior to anything my former gym offered, and the freedom to pick the length of my membership means I won't be sweating over money issues.

Ease Stress with Affordable Spa Treatments

Handy Home Spa Treatments

I was about to enjoy a deliciously indulgent facial at a local beauty school (much cheaper than an upscale salon) when the woman doing my treatment slathered my hands in rich creamy lotion, put each hand in a clear plastic bag and inserted each hand into its own heated mitt to help the hand lotion absorb more effectively. After my hands were tucked into the nice, cozy heated mitts, the esthetician proceeded to give my face the kind of serious pampering that melts stress and makes me want to make facials part of my daily routine.

Since I can't take the esthetician with the magic hands home with me, and frequent beauty treatments can add up, even at beauty school prices, I started thinking about how I could duplicate this pampering beauty treatment at home. Like the beauty treatments you get at a salon, you can customize your treatment to your own needs and preferences.

Start by creating the kind of mellow environment you find at a spa. Put on some relaxing instrumental music, and infuse your bedroom--or whatever space in your home is private and quiet--with soothing aromatherapy scents. I prefer scented reed diffusers because I can close my eyes without worrying about a candle lighting something on fire. Gather your supplies--hand lotion, two plastic bags, and two oven mitts--on a table near the bed. Now you are ready to begin.

Unlike the spa, your beauty treatment starts with the face, not the hands. In front of your bathroom mirror, apply the face mask of your choice, one that takes at least 20 minutes to work.

Lie down on the bed or couch. Slather your hands with a rich body or hand lotion. Insert each hand into a plastic bag to prevent lotion from rubbing off onto the oven mitts. Place each hand in an oven mitt. Now lie back and relax for about 20 minutes.

Some beauty experts may argue that face masks don't really do anything. I think they are missing the point of this exercise. The real purpose of this pampering is to relax and focus on the feeling of being indulged, if only for a short time. The mental benefits of pampering are just as important, if not more important, than the physical benefits.

How to Undress for Spa Treatments

Whether you are being pampered at a fancy salon or a local beauty school, dressing appropriately enhances the whole indulgent experience. When receiving any kind of spa treatment, what you don't wear is just as important as what you do wear. Leave expensive jewelry at home. Earrings and necklaces will either have to be removed or they will get mucked up by beauty products. At some spas you may have to leave your clothes in a closet or locker. Not bringing jewelry with you means you can relax and enjoy your treatments without worrying about your unattended jewelry being stolen.

Some treatments, such as facials, generally don't require you to undress much. You may need to remove your shirt and be given the option of removing your bra. I recommend removing your bra, since a facial often involves applying products to the upper chest and possibly shoulder area. Removing a bra makes it easier for the esthetician to work. (It also means I don't have to reveal my love of trashy lingerie to a virtual stranger.)

Anything you wear to a day spa or salon should be easy to remove. Struggling with straps or fastenings is not going to put you in a mellow spa-worthy frame of mind. Wear slip-on shoes for quick changes and a scoop-neck or V-neck T-shirt that is easy to pull on and off, or wear a shirt that unbuttons completely down the front. Wear clothes with a relaxed fit, like yoga pants.

Massage and facial oils don't always absorb completely into the skin, so some of that oil may end up on your clothes. Fabrics made with natural fibers like cotton will allow your skin to breathe, while synthetic fabrics will make you feel stickier.

If you have your handbag in the room with you during treatments, be sure to turn your cell phone off. Aside from a fire alarm, nothing is more jarring and disruptive than the sound of a ringing phone when you are trying to chill out and enjoy some much-needed pampering. It's time to put the world on hold for a while and fully enjoy the feeling of someone taking care of you.

Certain types of facials that remove dead skin cells can leave your skin vulnerable to the sun's rays for several hours after treatment. Don't schedule a facial before a day of running around outdoors for any length of time. If you are concerned about exposure to the sun, bring a wide-brimmed hat to wear outside after treatment. Facial treatments are typically designed to clear the pores and let them breathe a little, so slathering on a heavy layer of sunscreen right after might not be appropriate.

Save Money on Massages

Massage therapists who work in fancy salons all have one thing in common. They had to put in many hours of hands-on training before getting their hands on a job at a reputable salon. To help students rack up those required hours, many schools of massage therapy make massage services available to the public.

You can often get a thoroughly relaxing massage at a school for a lot less than you would pay at a salon or spa. What you won't get is a long list of choices in the type of massage you receive. While there are many different types of massage, one provided by a student is most likely to be pretty basic. Don't expect a lot of additional elements like hot stones or other special salon treatments. Of course, it couldn't hurt to ask the school's operator what services are available when you call for an appointment. To find a massage school in your area, check out massageregister.com.

For the kind of serious pampering that includes more specialized treatments found only at high-end salons and spas, check local salon and spa Web sites for specials and package deals. Also check local newspapers and magazines around gift-giving holidays like Mother's Day for advertised specials and coupons.

Be sure to allow plenty of time for your massage. Massages are such a wonderfully relaxing experience that some people fall asleep while getting one, and your massage therapist might be reluctant to wake you from your sweet dreams.

>>>>>>>>>>>>>>>>>>>>><<<<<<<<<<<<<<<<<<<<<

Recommended Reading

Looking Younger: Makeovers That Make You Look as Young as You Feel, by Robert Jones, offers plenty of practical advice for women interested in easy strategies for looking their best. The book offers simple solutions (such as disguising laugh lines and scars with concealer) for many common beauty issues. The models tend to look airbrushed, but I have to give Jones credit for including models in their 40s all the way up to their 70s. Airbrushed or not, the makeup looks natural and flattering.

The 5-Minute Face, by Carmindy, is a practical guide to looking fabulous fast. Makeup artist Carmindy demonstrates quick and easy makeup techniques that can be completed in five minutes. Once you have mastered the five-minute face, try one of her other makeup looks, like the slightly more dramatic yet very wearable holiday face. Carmindy also covers beauty topics such as shaping your brows, finding the right foundation, makeup as it applies to different age groups, and more.

The Original Beauty Bible, by Paula Begoun, cuts through the confusing hype and misinformation surrounding cosmetics and beauty products so consumers can spend smarter and treat their skin better. This comprehensive book tells you which cosmetic and skin care ingredients are effective, ineffective, or irritating. Begoun offers advice on many skin care topics, including solutions for acne, dry skin, and rosacea; hair removal; choosing flattering makeup colors; and more. Begoun also devotes a section to both the risks and rewards of various medical cosmetic procedures.

>>>>>>>>>>>>>>>>>>>>><<<<<<<<<<<<<<<<<<<<<

Part Four: Home Decor

"Have nothing in your house you do not know to be useful or believe to be beautiful."

--William Morris

Have a Seat: Furnishing Your Nest

Gilt by Association

While taking an interior-design class, I learned many lessons in style, most of which I have since forgotten. However, the lesson I learned on making affordable furnishings look rich was simply unforgettable. The instructor shared her secret to creating an upscale look by revealing the clever way she displayed her collection of bargain-priced clocks--all on the same wall, with one rare and expensive clock hung right in the center. Her guests never suspected the collection was mostly affordable mass-produced pieces. They assumed all the clocks were valuable because that one truly valuable clock lent an air of importance and elegance to the other clocks.

The affluent by association approach to decorating opens up a world of possibilities. Instead of limiting your display of collectibles to decorative eye candy meant to be touched and not used, why not display stuff you actually use as if it were a valuable collectible? Some well-designed, oven-friendly, and microwave-safe baking dishes or refrigerator-ready pitchers can be as posh as they are practical. A china cabinet filled with elegant dishes designed for everyday use mixed in with actual collectible dishes similar in style strongly implies that everything in the cabinet is a valuable collectible. The closer in style the collectibles are to the everyday dishes, the stronger the illusion.

Framing an ordinary object by attaching it to something exquisite elevates the look of that object. A cheap pillar candle resting on top of a beautiful candlestick complements the candlestick without cheapening the look of it. Artsy postcards picked up at a museum shop for a few bucks look like a million bucks when placed inside elegant matted frames, then arranged on a wall or table in a stylish manner.

A simple monogram added to plush bath towels or a nice bed throw adds a nice personal touch as well as a touch of class to your decor. A plain bed throw looks like an ordinary blanket until you add a monogram and place the throw across the bottom of the bed, neatly folded on top of the bedspread with the monogram displayed, thereby creating a five-star hotel effect. Wait for great deals on towels and bed throws so you can splurge on a fine monogramming job done by a local embroidery company. By including a few rich touches to your home decor, you can easily create the feeling of living in luxury every day, even on a modest budget.

Form Follows Function and Frugality in Decorating

For me, interior decorating is a creative process that simply boils down to asking the right questions until you get a satisfying answer. Questions like, "Do I really want to spend more on a couch than I do on my mortgage?" can lead to some pretty creative solutions. One of my favorite strategies for decorating on the cheap is to look at an affordable object and imagine it in my home serving a purpose it wasn't originally designed for.

When I came across a clearance-priced set of three nesting tables with solid panels on all four sides, I immediately saw their potential. I knew the nesting tables could easily be stacked and rearranged to suit my mood and my decor. I turned two of the tables on their sides, stacked one on top of the other and used this as a bedside table. The third table acts as a storage cube that sits on the floor displaying books and decorative items.

I had such a hard time finding stylish yet affordable curtains for my bedroom windows that I resorted to hanging an attractive pair of solid-color shower curtains in the bedroom. When I noticed the curtains didn't block the bright morning sunlight, I hung gray shower curtain liners behind them to block out the light and preserve my precious beauty sleep. I hung the curtains with decorative silvery metal shower curtain hooks. The fact that the shower curtains didn't quite reach the floor was easily disguised by putting furniture in front of the curtains. A chest in front of one window and a nightstand in front of the other hid the gap between the bottom of the curtain and the floor quite nicely.

In order to avoid cramping my budget, a lot of my furniture falls into the cheaper, "some assembly required" category, but I don't let that cramp my style. I have stacked a couple of faux wood-grain storage cubes on top of each other to serve as an end table. A TV stand in a brown wood slightly darker than the storage cubes serves as an end table on the other end of the couch. By seeing potential in these affordable furnishings, I gave myself more options than if I'd limited myself to buying actual end tables.

Narrow media storage towers about four feet high work beautifully in small spaces. In a well-ventilated bathroom the tower could hold toiletries, washcloths, and rolls of toilet paper. Next to the kitchen or dining area, the tower could be put to use to hold mugs, cocktail napkins, or extra glasses, freeing up kitchen cabinet space while keeping things you need easily accessible.

I'm not always 100 percent awake first thing in the morning, so it's important that my cosmetics are organized in a way that prevents me from accidentally trying to use that purple eye shadow cream as a lipstick. On my bathroom counter cosmetics are separated into three clear acrylic glasses. One glass holds lipsticks; another holds eye products like mascara, eyeliner, and an eyebrow pencil; and the third glass holds makeup brushes. With this system I can quickly identify and grab the products I need.

An attractive bed sheet also makes an attractive tablecloth. Sheets come in such a variety of patterns and colors that there is a style and price to suit every taste and table. For a richer look, layer a solid-color tablecloth under a lace tablecloth. Machine washable blankets and quilts give a warm, cozy feeling to the table. When decorating with an eye toward function and frugality is done well, it results in a more interesting and original take on home decor.

Mirrored Furniture Reflects a Passion for Style

I love using mirrored furniture for the sparkle and glamour it adds. Mirrored furniture looks rich and fabulous even when it comes from budget-friendly retailers such as Target, zgallerie.com, or Pier 1 Imports. To prevent my rooms from looking like a disco ball exploded inside them, I limit myself to a few mirrored pieces per room.

A mirrored piece of furniture can either expand the feeling of the room or double the visual clutter, depending on what it's reflecting. A mirrored chest sitting on a light-beige solid-color carpet creates a light, open effect with little visual interruption.

A mirrored piece of furniture sitting on a busy patterned rug reflects the pattern, resulting in a busy, cluttered look.

Unlike conventional wood furniture, mirrored furniture doesn't need to coordinate with other furniture in terms of matching upholstery or wood grain, which increases its versatility. Using silver accents near mirrored furniture subtly integrates it into the room's decor. On top of my mirrored chest I placed a deep plum scarf to protect the surface. On top of that I have a simple, streamlined music player in silver. Small accents throughout the room, like silver curtain hooks, silver drawer pulls on furniture pieces, and a wall clock with a silver frame, also tie in the mirrored chest to the rest of the room.

Like a pair of killer high heels, mirrored furniture pieces are designed for looks, not wear and tear. If the furniture piece is mirrored on top, placing a table runner or something else between objects and the mirrored surface prevents scratching. Arranging mirrored pieces against a wall in a low-traffic area reduces the chances of their being scratched or banged up. If the piece is used for storage, stock it with rarely used items. Less handling means you will seldom have to engage in the unglamorous task of wiping off fingerprints.

Painted Furniture Adds Pizzazz

Conventional decorating wisdom says you should buy larger furniture pieces in safe neutrals so you won't have to live with your mistake for years after the novelty of owning a hot pink plaid couch disappears. Playing it safe may seem smart, but it can be boring. An easy way to introduce bold colored furniture into your decor is to buy painted furniture.

An entire set of painted furniture works beautifully outdoors. With outdoor furniture there usually isn't an entire room filled with carpets and painted walls to coordinate with, so you have a lot more creative freedom. If the furniture feels a little too bright, tone it down a little with outdoor cushions in white or other neutral colors.

A single piece of painted furniture indoors creates an eye-catching focal point. A bright blue bench or table in the entrance hall offers a cheerful welcome. By repeating that same shade of blue on patterned pillows or decorative vases in an adjoining room, the painted furniture ties into other areas of the home without the spaces being saturated with lots of bright color. A small bookcase or cabinet in a brilliant color also adds a bit of personality to a room. If the novelty of owning a neon green bookcase ever wears off, you can always repaint it.

Pillow Talk

Pillows are the quick change artists of home decor, adding personality to a room for very little cost. When shopping for pillows, think about how the pillows relate to the furniture they are resting on and the overall look of the room. It's easy to find stylish pillows through such retailers as Target, Bed Bath & Beyond, or Crate & Barrel.

Pillows can add visual interest to a room by introducing a strong color, pattern, texture, or a bit of whimsy. For a room that already has enough pattern and color, solid-color pillows in subdued shades give the eye somewhere to rest amid the more attention-grabbing elements. Patterned pillows that include colors from different pieces in the room pull a look together by relating these elements to one another.

For fun, toss a statement pillow, one with a witty saying or design printed or embroidered on it, into an otherwise elegantly decorated room. This shows guests that while you take your personal style very seriously, you don't take yourself too seriously.

Bringing Outdoor Furnishings Inside

In recent years, outdoor furnishings have started to imitate indoor furnishings so closely it can look like you moved your living room outside with the birds and the bugs! The problem with this trend is that the outdoor space needs to be enclosed or at least covered for this "outdoor living room" to remain outdoors year round.

Good quality outdoor furnishings are too expensive to be just fair-weather friends. Instead of trying to bring your indoor style outside temporarily, why not bring outdoor furniture inside and put it to use? Bistro furniture, with its small tables and coordinating folding chairs, could easily be adapted for indoor use during the cooler months. Create your own mini bistro by placing the table and chair set near the kitchen, or use the bistro set for extra seating during parties.

Folding chairs originally designed for the outdoors can be put to use as extra chairs for parties any time of the year. Do your guests a favor and add a seat cushion, and artfully drape a blanket or beach towel over the back of the chair to add a layer of comfortable padding and a dash of style. Shop lawn and garden centers, as well as mass retailers, for outdoor furniture that works year round.

When the change of seasons brings reduced daylight hours, it's time to bring some of those solar lights you used to light up the night for fun summer gatherings indoors. Set solar lights on a windowsill so they can absorb the sun's rays all day, and come evening, you will have a portable source of light that illuminates your space for hours on end. How's that for a bright idea in making your furnishings go farther!

Invisible Decorating in the Bathroom

The challenge with small bathrooms is that so many items need to be close at hand, yet having all that stuff on display creates visual clutter that can make the space look smaller than it actually is. One way of dealing with this problem would be to give up some of my beauty products which, trust me, would not be pretty. I found a better way of dealing with this dilemma is to make fixtures and towels blend into the background.

I use a clear acrylic shelving unit that literally disappears into the wall. I display beauty products in attractive packaging on the shelves to add some color to an otherwise bland space. Displaying a limited selection of products you actually use in an attractive way is a practical solution to the lack of space in the bathroom issue.

One of the nicest gifts I ever received were some fluffy cream-color towels with my initials embroidered on them. I hung them in the bathroom from clear acrylic towel holders attached to the wall. The cream-color walls made the towels do a disappearing act, making the bathroom look less cluttered and more spacious. The light-color towels feature a black monogram, which adds some visual interest by sharply contrasting against all that cream. A bit of color or pattern here and there prevents a plain white bathroom from feeling as cold and impersonal as an igloo.

Shower Curtains for Small Spaces

Shower curtains have a huge impact on the look and feel of a bathroom. The right shower curtain creates a more spacious feel in the bathroom. Vertical patterns such as stripes and climbing vines add visual height to the room, distracting attention from the overall lack of space. A light-color shower curtain set against a background of light-color walls and a white tub provides a sense of continuity. On the other hand, a sharp contrast between the tub and shower curtain visually divides the space horizontally, making it look smaller. Bed Bath & Beyond has a great selection of reasonably priced shower curtains, and it frequently sends out coupons to customers who sign up for its mailing list.

Coordinating bath towels with the shower curtain creates a more pulled-together look for the bathroom. If your towels are a mismatched bunch, invest in a neutral shower curtain, like a subdued--not shiny--metallic silver, gold, or copper-color fabric. With a few new towels or decorative accessories you can change the color scheme of the bathroom instantly without having to replace the shower curtain.

Room for Improvement: Easy Organizing Ideas

Free and Cheap Ways to Get Organized

When it comes to getting organized, your first impulse may be to run out to the store and stock up on containers. This is a popular procrastination technique since shopping is a lot more fun than staying at home and dealing with piles of stuff. A cheaper way to approach the whole organizing thing is to skip the stores and shop your own home for free organizers.

The first step is to do a clean sweep, getting rid of stuff you don't use and--let's face it--you really don't want. Once these objects have been removed from your home, you won't be tempted to spend money on organizing containers simply to keep stuff out of sight. A leaky pipe under the sink in my bathroom forced me to remove a pile of grooming-related paraphernalia. I was surprised at how much stuff ended up not going back under the sink after the pipe was fixed. Worthless stuff went in the trash, and useful stuff I no longer wanted was donated to a thrift store.

As I get rid of stuff, I take a moment to look at the container it was in and imagine possible new uses for that container. When I was going through my closet and came across a pair of shoes in practically new condition that I had no interest in wearing, I kept the plastic shoe box they had been stored in and donated the shoes to the local thrift store. The shoebox now contains and protects my beauty products in the bathroom cabinet under the sink.

Other free containers to consider are packaging materials from things you have bought. Clear zippered plastic bags that your bed linens came in are great for storing sweaters or other stuff under your bed. It's a shame to throw out pretty beauty cream jars. Instead of trashing perfectly good jars, save the ones with a wide opening at the top and give your desk drawer or your junk drawer a touch of glamour by using them to corral small items like paper clips or thumb tacks.

While you are making a clean sweep of your home, don't forget the kitchen. Behind cabinet doors may be a wealth of useful organizing containers. An attractive glass or mug that isn't part of a set can be put to use as a pencil holder. A small bowl or sugar container could act as a convenient key holder on a counter or near a doorway. A decorative napkin holder could prevent bills from taking over your kitchen table by keeping them neatly contained.

Painless Room Planning

Furniture planning would be a breeze if it wasn't for a few minor details, like windows and doors in the most inconvenient places. If major renovations are out of the question, try mapping the location of furniture before arranging it in the room to help you avoid having to shuffle your furniture around like a deck of cards. Planning the location of your furniture before moving into a new space may alert you that some of your furniture might not fit into that space or let you know how much space you will have to add new pieces of furniture to the room.

If you are moving furniture into an empty space and you just want a quick way to figure out where to put what, grab a newspaper. Measure the pieces of furniture destined to go into that room and record the length and width of each piece in a notebook. With a pencil, ruler, and cellophane tape, cut the sheets down to size or tape them together to match the length and width of pieces of furniture. Write the name of each piece of furniture--"couch," for example--in bold letters on the newspaper. When you have a newspaper template for every piece of furniture going into that room, arrange and rearrange the templates in the empty room until you are satisfied. Leave the templates on the floor for reference until you move the actual pieces of furniture into the room. This process can also be done with cheap butcher paper, found at arts and crafts stores.

For a more high-tech approach that works on both empty and fully furnished rooms, try an online room arranger. On Better Homes and Gardens' Web site, you can find a room arranger that allows you to take into account the size of the room and different structural elements such as doors that swing into the room (click on "Home Improvement," "Home Design Tools," and "Arrange a Room" at bhg.com). The drawings representing different pieces of furniture help give you a more realistic feel for how the furniture will look in a room. It takes a while to put everything into the virtual room, but it sure beats hauling a heavy armoire all over a room in real life trying to figure out where it fits.

For a low-tech, hands-on approach, try furniture sliders, small coasters that fit under furniture legs to make it easier to move the furniture around. The sliders have a smooth surface on the bottom that allows you to push your furniture around without having to lift it.

When you start to plan the arrangement of your furniture, take into account things like traffic flow and convenience. A table next to a chair is a convenient place for a guest to set down drinks or a book. Furniture placed almost directly in the path of a door disrupts the flow of traffic. Once you know how to arrange furniture, those awkwardly placed windows won't get in the way of you creating a comfortable, welcoming space.

The Cheap Diva Cleans Up Her Act

Housework can be ugly business, but it doesn't have to be. With the right approach, housework can enhance your appearance and your mind. The first step to tackling housework with style is to dress the part. If you clean with cheap, nontoxic cleaners, such as one part vinegar mixed with one part water, instead of harsh chemicals or bleaching agents, you won't have to dress in rags. A properly fitting T-shirt, stretch pants, and slip-on flats are comfortable enough to work in and cute enough to answer the door in. The deliveryman does not need to know what you look like at your frumpiest.

When cleaning in the kitchen rub some olive oil on your hands before putting on rubber gloves. Make your hair shine brighter than a polished faucet by applying a conditioning treatment to your hair while cleaning the bathroom with nontoxic cleaners. Continue to clean the bathtub and bathroom for the amount of time the hair treatment is supposed to be in and then take a shower, rinsing away the bathtub cleaner and the hair conditioner.

Incorporate exercise moves as you work, like squats and lunges while reaching down or vacuuming. Stretching when dusting helps you keep in shape while keeping your home in tip-top shape. If the housework at hand is not strenuous enough to exercise your body, you can still exercise your mind. Many audio books and entertaining podcasts are available as digital downloads that can play while you work. If the audio book is really engrossing, like a suspense novel, save it for a mindless, time-consuming task. For quick chores, turn on a language audio book and learn to speak like a native, not a tourist. Most audio language sets break down the learning process into small, manageable parts so it can be stopped and started to suit your cleaning schedule.

Sometimes the best way to approach a home in serious need of cleaning is to use your imagination to entertain yourself. Imagine that you are a spy (on the run from the fashion police. You should have known better than to wear white shoes with dark hose) posing as house sitter. Everything needs to be cleaned and organized so when the “real” owners return they are not aware of your deception. If you get carried away with your intricate plots, keep a journal of your “adventures” to reread later for your own amusement. Sure it’s silly, but isn’t it better to feel a little silly than a lot stressed out about all the work you have to do?

Shopping Strategies for the Home

Furnish Your Nest with Less Stress

To avoid costly home decor disasters, take a few moments to develop a strategy that increases your chances of getting it right the first time. Determine your objectives for the piece of furniture you want to acquire. If you are shopping for a couch, for example, do you want a couch long enough to lie down on for naps, or a smaller couch that leaves room for a group of chairs that can be easily rearranged for different leisure time activities?

How long do you want the piece to last? If your lodgings are temporary or other things take precedence in your budget, like saving up for a home nice enough to be worthy of fine furnishings, then it's perfectly fine to buy cheap furniture that is designed more for looks than heirloom potential.

A piece of furniture not only needs to fit your personality and your style, it also needs to fit into your home! Take careful measurements and record them in a small notebook to take furniture shopping with you. Measure the area the piece of furniture needs to fit into. For example, if you are trading in your old bed for larger one and it has to squeeze in between already existing bedside tables, measure the space between those tables. Now measure the doorways, stairways, and halls that the piece of furniture will have to pass through to get to its final location.

Before hitting the stores, hit the books, or magazines if that's easier. Clip pictures of pieces of furniture and put them in a notebook to take with you shopping. Showing the salesperson a picture of the styles you like will save you from aimlessly wandering around the store until you are so exhausted you are tempted to take a nap in the mattress department. More helpful items to put in your look book before heading out to the stores are paint samples from the room the furniture is going in, fabric swatches of other pieces of furniture in the room, or slipcovers from pillows or chair cushions.

If you find the perfect piece at a great price, go ahead and measure the width, length, and height of it. Record these measurements in your notebook and check them against the measurements you took of your stairways, halls, etc. Ideally, you'll need at least a few inches of extra space between your furniture and the areas it has to pass through.

When you find a piece that has potential, but you're not convinced it's the best piece or the best price you can find, record the brand, model, price, dimensions, and salesperson's name for future reference. If you decide after much serious thought and fruitless shopping that you want that piece after all, you'll have all the information you need to call the store and verify that the piece is still in stock. Or you can use this information to shop for it online and do some price comparisons while you're at it.

The Art of Negotiation

Want a better deal on your home furnishings? Just ask for it. When negotiating for a better deal, start by approaching the seller with confidence. Signs of a confident attitude include good posture (no slouching), making eye contact, and asking questions in a friendly tone of voice. This is a business transaction, so don't reveal how badly you want the item by acting like an overenthusiastic shopaholic who just set eyes on a fabulous prize.

When requesting a better deal, get to the point quickly and be specific in your request. Don't ask vague question such as, "Do you do discounts?" Certain types of merchandise might be open to negotiation, while others are not. A more specific question along the lines of, "What kind of deal can you give me on this painting of dogs playing poker?" will allow the seller to give you a more specific answer. Always treat the person you are talking to with respect. Do not try to pressure him or her into giving you a better deal by making nasty remarks about the merchandise and adopting the attitude that you are somehow doing the store a favor by taking it off its hands. Do not make ridiculous demands like asking for 75 percent off the price of an item. Unless the current price is horribly inflated or the item has been sitting around so long it's practically a relic, something along the lines of 10 to 20 percent off is generally considered a reasonable request.

When negotiating for a lower price, it helps to give the seller a good reason for lowering the price. Many sellers are willing to match prices with another store as long as the item is the same brand and the same style of an item being sold. When my old mattress got so worn it started poking me in the back with a loose spring, I decided that while buying a new mattress might put a dent in my budget, it was essential for my beauty sleep. The first store I looked at offered free shipping and a bed frame with each mattress. I wanted to do a little comparison shopping, so I went to another store, where I found the perfect mattress. The second store didn't offer free delivery or a free bed frame with the mattress I wanted. I happened to have the business card from the first mattress store, so I whipped out my cell phone while sitting on my dream mattress and called the other store. After I verified that the first store still had the free delivery and frame promotion going on, the salesperson at the second store deducted the cost of delivery and the bed frame from my bill, which saved me enough cash to cover the cost of a new set of sheets.

Another good reason to ask for a discount is if the piece happens to be flawed or missing something. Furniture that needs a little work can be a great deal as long as the flaws are easily fixed. For example, if the antique chest of drawers is missing some drawer pulls, you could mention to the sellers that you are going to have to buy a whole new set of drawer pulls, and then ask them how much they would be willing to deduct from the price.

Sellers often prefer payments of cash. It doesn't hurt to ask, "If I pay in cash now, what kind of discount can you give me?" This strategy works better with independent stores. It probably won't work at your local Wal-Mart.

If a seller isn't able to come down in price, maybe he can throw in something for free. I know one enlightened shopper who got a pair of free lamps to go with the living room couch and chairs she and her husband had just bought simply by asking the salesman if he would throw in the lamps for free. Because a living room set is an expensive purchase, and the lamps were comparatively cheap, the salesman saw this as a perfectly reasonable request that was going to make his valuable customers very happy.

When the seller refuses to give you a discount, accept his or her decision graciously and continue shopping around, or fork over the full asking price if it's something you truly want and can afford. Don't badger the seller into trying to give you a better deal after he has said no. It doesn't pay to be rude.

Discount Stores Offer Stylish Home Décor

Once upon a time I went shopping at the local T.J. Maxx looking for stylish drinking glasses. I left the store with some cooking pans, an exercise DVD, and a decorative memo board, but no glasses. It's just that kind of store. Stores like T.J. Maxx and Marshalls sell discontinued or overstocked items at discounted prices--everything from bedding to dishes, to decorative accents, to lamps, furniture, and a variety of other home-related goods. Because the stock they carry comes from a variety of sources, the quality of the products will vary.

The reward for wading through this eclectic collection of home goods is that you can often find great deals on some seriously stylish stuff. The trick is to keep an open mind and look at everything, and I do mean everything, in the home decor department. Because they deal in discontinued goods, different stores will carry different merchandise.

These stores also sell clothing, but from what I've seen it's pretty hard to find cute stuff in popular sizes (anything above a size 4). T.J. Maxx and Marshalls don't sell online at this time. Personally I think it's more fun to wander the aisles in search of the unexpected gem than stare at a computer screen, but that's just me.

Buying Home Decor Items on eBay

Shopping on eBay is the ultimate treasure hunt. The trick is to separate the trash from the treasure. When shopping for home decor items on eBay always pay attention to the wording to be sure you really understand what you are buying. Items listed as "retro" or "vintage style" may be a copy of a vintage item. There is nothing wrong with buying a copy; there is just no reason to pay top dollar for a reproduction that can be produced in unlimited quantities as opposed to a genuine vintage item where quantities are limited.

Be aware of alterations that have been made to the item before you buy. I once found a blue vintage camera that I thought was some sort of extremely rare limited edition. I read the description and found out the seller had taken a common vintage camera and painted it blue. It was not a rare item and therefore not as valuable.

For three-dimensional objects the seller should show pictures of the objects from different angles. If the pictures are inadequate, e-mail the seller and ask for more pictures before bidding. Not everything in the picture is always included in the sale. The person selling a vintage microphone might photograph it on a microphone stand that is not included, for instance.

Pictures can also give a misleading impression of size. Those sculptures that look so dramatic in the picture can turn out to be disappointingly dinky knickknacks when you receive them and open the box. Get measurements and read the seller's description before bidding. Because of the expensive shipping and handling costs, eBay is not the best place to shop for furniture, but it is great for finding the kind of unique home decor items that you won't find at the local mall.

Don't Do It Yourself

Years ago I snatched up a solid wood buffet, also referred to as a side table, for a mere $20 at a local thrift store. The old buffet was covered in a layer of horrid light blue paint. I was confident that once the blue paint was removed I would be left with an elegant buffet that would enhance my living space, and I was right. All it took to bring out the beauty in this bargain were some paint stripping materials, a lovely deep rich wood stain, and over $200 to pay someone far more skilled in woodworking than I am to do the job!

When I purchased the buffet I had visions of popping into the local hardware store to pick up a few supplies, stripping it, and slapping on some wood stain on a lazy afternoon. When I found out what would be involved in turning this light blue eyesore into brag-worthy home decor it was clear I needed professional help. I've had the buffet for years, and it still looks great, but that was the last time I bought fixer-upper furniture with the intention of turning it into a do-it-myself project.

Before buying anything in need of a makeover, ask yourself if you have the skills needed to repair, refinish, or reupholster the item. If the answer is no, are you genuinely interested in learning the skills needed to transform the object? If you're not the do-it-yourself type and you don't want to spend hundreds of dollars hiring someone, then focus on finding objects that are right for you right now, no makeover needed.

Fresh Flowers Bloom at Local Farmers' Markets

Local farmers' markets have evolved over the years to provide much more than fresh produce. Popular farmers' markets offer live music, cooking demonstrations, and fresh flowers. Like the fruit and vegetables sold at farmers' markets, you can expect the flower selection to change with the seasons. For a longer-lasting bouquet, look for flowers that haven't quite fully bloomed, with fully developed, unopened heads. Ideally, fresh flowers will blossom and reveal their true beauty in the comfort of your home.

To get your pick of the prettiest flowers, shop early, before the best bouquets get snatched up. If getting first pick isn't a concern, you may get a better deal toward the end of the day. Bring a tote bag with a shoulder strap with you and stash your farmers' market finds in the bag, leaving your hands free to carry your bouquet. This way you can literally stop and smell the roses as you stroll leisurely through the market.

Make Yourself at Home: Developing an Eye for Design

Coming Out of the Closet

If you're a stylish dresser but stumped about how to express your sense of style in your home decor, look to your clothing and accessories for inspiration. Look at the pieces in your closet that are personal favorites, and think about how you put them together to create an outfit. The colors and patterns in your closet can often be translated into paint colors, upholstery materials, and fabric accents such as curtains and pillows.

A typical outfit might consist of neutral color pants topped off by a sweater or blouse in a contrasting color or texture. Accessories may include shoes with an interesting heel and some super-shiny jewelry. How does this translate into a room such as a bedroom? The neutral pants can provide inspiration for a basic investment piece such as a nice bedspread in a neutral gray or brown. The color of the blouse can provide inspiration for less prominent fabrics such as sheets and pillowcases. If the texture of the blouse was a knit, this could easily translate into knit jersey sheets or a cozy knit blanket tossed on the bed or a chair.

The heel of a shoe suggests an interest in sculptural elements. Look for chairs or end tables, lamps, and other decorative accessories that have straight or curved lines similar to your most stylish heels. Your favorite jewelry provides the inspiration for decorative accents. Go for the gold with a mirror surrounded by a gold frame, or add gold-color drawer pulls to the dressers and desk in the room. Show off your sterling sense of style with gleaming accents such as pictures with silver frames, silver candlesticks, or lamps with a silver base. The same instincts that serve you so well when you wear stylish clothes that fit your personality can help you create a signature style for your rooms.

Create Your Own Home Decor Magazine

Home decor magazines brimming with well-decorated and, in some cases, over-decorated rooms, provide inspiration and hope to those of us living in more humble dwellings. I enjoy clipping pictures from these magazines with the intention that someday I will imitate some aspect of the home or room featured on their glossy pages in my own home.

When I started going through my pile of magazine pictures, I wondered what I had been thinking when I clipped a picture of a badly decorated room in desperate need of a complete makeover. Was I interested in the way the pictures were arranged on a wall or the furniture layout in the room, or had I just lost my mind? After one too many "lost my mind" moments, I created my own home decor magazine of sorts. I bought a cheap binder, the kind you find at office supply stores, and lots of clear 8.5-by-11-inch plastic sleeves. As I clipped pictures from magazines I put them in the sleeves inside the binder.

Here are a few pointers on creating your own look book:

- Grouping images by theme makes it easier to grasp what the picture is referencing. If I am interested in window treatments, I group them in adjacent sleeves, even if the one picture features a bedroom and another features a living room.

- Look past the "wow" factor when looking at pictures in magazines. A room may not dazzle you with its beauty, yet certain elements, such as furniture layout, paint color, window treatments, or the arrangements of vases and other home accessories, may appeal to you.
- Write notes about changes you would make to the room on the picture itself or on a sticky note slipped inside the clear binder sleeve holding the picture. If you like the way a group of botanical prints is arranged on a wall but would prefer classic movie posters instead, make a note of it.
- Don't limit your look book to magazine pictures. Add a clear plastic zip-up pencil pouch to your binder. Use it to hold fabric swatches or paint-color samples from the hardware store.
- At the back of the binder, behind all the glossy pictures of fantasy rooms, insert some of those plain binder pockets, also sold at office supply stores, for storing articles on related subjects like wall-painting techniques, the proper hardware for hanging different types of pictures, or any other home DIY projects.

A personalized decorating book like this is a wonderful reference for home decorating projects, and it's also a fun and easy way to develop your own sense of style.

McMansions on Parade

Years of enjoying the free, open-to-the-public semiannual home tours sponsored by local home builders has made me something of a free home tour connoisseur. The interiors of the deluxe homes designed by professional interior designers provide plenty of design inspiration. Looking at too many luxury homes in a row causes all the homes to blend into one big faux Italian villa/overstuffed couch/beige wall/walk-in closet McMansion blur, so I limit the number of homes I tour in one day. By selecting about seven of the most expensive furnished homes listed to tour, I come away feeling inspired, not exhausted.

A brochure for the tour of homes, complete with an extremely vague and misleading map, usually appears in the Sunday paper shortly before the tours starts. I always make a point of printing out pages from the home tour's Web site that include detailed directions to the various houses. When I rely solely on the brochure map, I end up lost, cruising aimlessly through expensive subdivisions. The residents of these upscale enclaves look at me in my outdated economy car as though I were scouting the neighborhood to steal something other than decorating ideas from their expensive homes.

Wear cheap slip-on shoes, since you may have to take them off at the entrance to each house. Now that you have entered the McMansion of your dreams, stop dreaming and start taking notes. These houses were decorated by professional interior designers. Carry a camera and little notebook to jot down ideas or do a rough sketch. Just don't get too snap-happy. Cameras are not always allowed in some of the more expensive homes.

Some of the grander homes will actually make you feel better about your own home. I have seen bathrooms in million-dollar homes smaller than the bathroom in the one-bedroom apartment I was living in, and backyards so small the view was dominated by the neighbor's air-conditioning unit ten feet away.

It's comforting to tour these huge homes and realize that living large doesn't always mean living better.

Save Some Dough When You Do It Yourself

When I hear the phrase "do it yourself," it conjures up images of low-budget home makeover shows where they attack a room with gallons of paint, a squad of carpenters, and a designer with over-the-top made-for-TV taste. When I took an introductory class on interior design, an important thing I learned was that there are many ways to express yourself by doing it yourself that don't involve a power saw or perky TV host.

If you want to turn your walls into a work of art, for example, local paint stores sometimes offer faux painting classes for free or a low charge to their customers. Check into the classes offered by your local hardware store; some may cover the types of projects you would like to tackle in your own home. I should note that many professional handymen and carpenters love do-it-yourselfers because a lot of their business comes from fixing the projects the amateurs screwed up. By starting off with simple, almost fool-proof projects, you will save yourself the cost and embarrassment of having to explain to a handyman exactly how your project turned into such a disaster.

Because craft and fabric stores are basically warehouse-size shrines for do-it-yourselfers, they often make a point of having classes geared toward decorating projects. I have found that one of the most useful decorating skills you can learn is sewing. For anyone who has gasped at the price of a $90 pillow or checked out the cost of decent curtains, a sewing class geared toward home decor is a better investment than that $90 pillow. For free instructions on countless home decor-related projects, visit Martha Stewart at marthastewart.com or head to your local library to check out some of its craft books.

The biggest benefit of learning a skill is that you have a much better chance of getting exactly what you want. Whatever do-it-yourself projects you decide to tackle, I promise you that the sense of satisfaction you get from a job well done is even more rewarding than the money you save.

Putting the Home in Home Office

The convenience and money-saving benefits of home offices makes them a popular alternative to having an office outside the home. The wonderful thing about a home office is that you can literally make yourself at home and create a working environment that is tailored to your personal needs. Sometimes space limitations may require you to combine your working space with some other type of living space. When a home office is part of a bedroom or living room, it's essential to integrate the office trappings into the decor in a way that doesn't look as if you have an office cubicle parked in your living room.

A stylish home office typically revolves around a desk. The bigger and bulkier the desk, the harder it is to integrate into the home decor. For my current home office I accidentally bought a console with two drawers, not realizing it wasn't a traditional desk. A console is narrower than a desk and often used in areas like hallways. This mistake turned out to be a happy accident because my home office is located in a bedroom. The narrow console blends in with the furnishings much better than a wider desk would have.

It's not necessary to buy a desk with drawers large enough to fit piles of business-related files. Cabinets and other containers to hold files allow for more flexibility in how you arrange your furniture in a room. You can find chic file cabinets designed to look like dressers that easily blend into the home environment. To keep smaller sets of files close at hand, look for stylish totes specifically designed to hold files wherever organizing supplies are sold. Or you can buy a roomy tote bag and insert a file holder inside it yourself.

No matter how stylish the furnishings, between printers, computers, and office supplies it's difficult to disguise the home-office aspect of a room completely. What you can do is downplay the office vibe by coordinating pieces in a way that says "harmonious home decor," not "hardworking home office." Buy furniture in coordinating colors that looks like home furniture, not office furniture.

One of the cheapest ways to make your home office feel homier is to reduce the amount of paper sitting around. There have been moments when it looked as if I collected papers as a hobby because I had so many piles of them. Once I started going through papers and organizing them into files or throwing them out, it not only improved the look of the room; it improved my productivity as well.

Holiday Decorating Complements Home Décor

Holidays present a chance to let loose and indulge in decorating whims, but holiday decorating should still reflect your personal sense of style, just like year round home decor. Holidays that emphasize decorating--I'm thinking of Halloween in particular--can sometimes give your home a split personality. My attitude is that if I don't normally include bloody, dismembered body parts in my home decor, why should I display them at Halloween? My preferred Halloween decorations tend to be more spooky and mysterious than gory. The silhouette of a black cat in the window or a deep red tablecloth with a black spider web fabric draped over it decorated with simple black dishes, for example, shows off my Halloween spirit without turning my home into a house of horrors.

If your style is generally streamlined and simple, don't bother buying a lot of Halloween stuff that would stay in storage most of the year. A black-and-white Halloween theme can include a few simple props scattered about. Everything from ghosts to skeletons to bats can add to the Halloween ambience without adding any colors that clash with your existing decor. White dishes on a black tablecloth can hold chocolate cookies in the shapes of bats, a black cat, or a witch's hat. Fat black pillar candles set the mood. If you desire a splash of additional color, add solid bright red or orange accents, such as napkins, into the mix.

If you would describe your favorite decorating style as cozy, and you are sentimental down to your soul, then just about anything with a handcrafted look enhances the warm, welcoming feel of your home. Go ahead and embrace traditional fall colors and themes such as scarecrows, pumpkins, and fall leaves. Warm spice colors, muted oranges, rich browns, and burgundies are more subtle and inviting than high-contrast color schemes like black and orange.

A splendid decorating look for those who prefer less gore, more glam would be an ornate Victorian style. Elegant candelabras draped with fake spider webs (yes, the spider webs are fake. I'm not that bad a housekeeper!) look spooky and elegant for Halloween and can be reused for other special occasions. Fancy vases filled with dying flowers, and ornate silver gravy boats or bowls are perfect for serving candy. Expand on the vintage haunted house look by buying old books at used book stores or thrift stores and stacking them under serving dishes to add height and variety to your table decor. A black lace shawl used as a tablecloth or draped across a window complements the look.

Consistency is important when creating a certain type of atmosphere. Eclectic styles, such as bloody gore alternating with cute smiling pumpkins, send mixed messages and cancel each other out. If distinctly different decorating styles appeal to you, decorate one room in one style and another room in another style.

Harmonious Holiday Decorations

When it comes to the holidays, it's easy to allow your personal sense of style to get lost among the traditional holiday decorating clichés. A massive Christmas tree buried under urgently blinking lights and a haphazard assortment of tasteful and tacky ornaments looks as out of place in an otherwise subdued and tasteful living room as Santa at an Easter egg hunt.

Holiday decorations should be as much a reflection of your personal style as the things you display year round. If your style is clean and contemporary, there is no reason your home should look as though a Hallmark store exploded in your living room.

A few festive accents here and there reflect the holiday spirit and your personal style. Displaying shiny ornaments gathered in a clear glass bowl or tied from a ribbon hanging between the posts of a stair railing can complement or completely replace a traditional Christmas tree.

Red and green are traditional holiday colors, but selecting ornaments and holiday decor that pick up on your already existing color scheme creates a more harmonious effect. A white flocked tree with blue and aqua ornaments, for example, complements a room where whites and blues are an essential part of the everyday decor.

If the very thought of massive holiday decorating makes you feel like a real Grinch, remember there are plenty of less clutter-prone ways to create a mood. A scented candle or reed diffuser strategically placed enhances the holiday mood. There is also plenty of holiday music that aims to be more soothing than some of the annoying holiday jingles we associate with the season. The holiday season is supposed to be a time of joy, so go ahead and decorate and celebrate in ways that are the most joyful to you.

>>>>>>>>>>>>>>>>>>>><<<<<<<<<<<<<<<<<<<<

Recommended Reading

Slob Proof!, by Debbie Wiener, offers design advice that tackles the reality of how you really live with humor and insight. Wiener's years of experience as a professional interior designer combined with her years of living with a husband and children who are slobs enables her to design living spaces that are both attractive and practical. Whether talking about wall paint, window coverings, floors, or furniture, the author emphasizes stain resistance, stain camouflage, practicality, and durability.

The House Always Wins, by Marni Jameson, is packed with humor and great decorating advice. Jameson takes the reader along with her as she navigates the confusing and often stressful process of building and decorating her house. Alongside her real-life stories of decorating disasters she includes plenty of advice from the experts on everything from picking carpeting to getting the correct drapery hardware to just about anything else an amateur decorator would need to know.

>>>>>>>>>>>>>>>>>>>><<<<<<<<<<<<<<<<<<<<

Part Five: Entertaining

"Tact is the art of making your guests feel at home when that's where you wish they really were."

--George Bergman

Be My Guest: Entertaining at Home

Hosting 101

Being a good host can be as simple as putting on a little background music, having some drinks and light refreshments ready, and greeting your guests with a warm smile. It's not hard, yet I have witnessed some truly awful examples of incompetent hosting.

At a social gathering at a friend's house, for example, instead of greeting me with a warm smile and offering me a drink, the hostess started off by complaining about how busy she was. When cookies and drinks were eventually served, the store-bought cookies were still in the grocery store container, which was still inside a grocery sack. She could have at least put them on a plate! Her behavior practically screamed, "Having guests is a major inconvenience, go away!" Here's a tip for the busy host: Don't greet your guests by complaining about how busy you are. Did you specify on the invitation that the social occasion was a pity party? No? Then stop complaining. It makes your guests feel unwanted.

Help guests feel welcome by making it easy for them to find your house. When guests arrive so late you are about ready to send out a search party to find them, maybe the problem isn't bad manners but bad directions. Include a map with the invitation or directions that shows obvious points of reference, like major intersections. House numbers are often difficult to spot, so make it easier for guests to identify your home by mentioning something distinctive about your home or landscaping. Christmas lights can set your house apart--especially if you are hosting a party in June.

Before guests arrive, set the mood with background music low enough that guests don't have to shout to be heard over the music. Either greet guests at the door with a warm smile yourself or have someone your guests are familiar with act as greeter. This alleviates concern from guests who visit so rarely they need some reassurance that they have indeed arrived at the right house.

Have a variety of drinks ready, and offer guests a beverage shortly after they arrive. Keep the first guest company while waiting for others to arrive. If you are in the middle of last-minute preparations when the first guests arrive, enlist their help with easy tasks and thank them graciously for their contribution. The first guest does not want to be abandoned in the living room like a social outcast while you are finishing up in the kitchen.

When offering a variety of food to a hungry crowd, spread the food out into different feeding stations. Stock one station with drinks and another with hot appetizers, while another station serves a selection of desserts, and so forth. This encourages guests to mingle and move about. It also prevents a pack of impatient guests from getting stuck in line at a single buffet table. While your guests are starving, someone at the head of the line will inevitably stand there like a statue, debating which high-calorie dishes are worth ruining the fad diet she's on this week.

Your carpet may be stain resistant, but guests aren't. Spare guests the hassle of juggling beverages and food plates by arranging tables within reach of any chair or couch. If your guests are gracious enough to clean up after themselves, let them! Have a small trash can available so guests can dispose of food accessories such as paper napkins, empty drink cans, or toothpicks. Being a good host is simply a matter of thinking ahead to create a welcoming environment full of warm smiles and no whining!

Getting-to-Know-You Games

In certain social situations where you are bringing together guests who might not know each other very well, "getting to know you games" make it fun and easy for everyone to relax and mingle. One great game is Two Truths and a Lie. Each guest takes turns making three brief statements about herself or himself. Two of those statements are true, and one is a lie. The other guests guess which one of the statements is the lie. The guests choose what personal information they share. Their major in college, a favorite food, a hobby, or one odd job that is completely different from a current career are all good topics.

It's not every day someone in the midst of a casual conversation turns to you and says, "Oh by the way, years ago a man held me at gunpoint, which resulted in a police standoff. Luckily, no one got hurt." It's not until you create a situation that invites everyone to share their more interesting stories that you find out how interesting your friends really are. A game called "What people don't know about me is…" encourages everyone to share a piece of interesting personal history.

This game works best with a group of eight to twelve. Arrange chairs in a circle so everyone can easily see and hear one another. Give everyone a small slip of paper and something to write with. Instruct guests to write one sentence. The sentence starts with "What people don't know about me is ____," and it's up to each guest to fill in the blank. Give guests a reasonable amount of time to think about one thing in their personal histories that the other people in the group are unaware of and to write it on the slip of paper. Once everyone is done writing, collect the slips of paper and put them in a bowl.

Pick one of the slips out of the bowl and read it out loud. When you read a slip saying "What people don't know about me is that in college I grew my hair long and dyed it blond so I could look good on stage in my role as lead singer for a local rock band," it's up to everyone in the group (except the person who wrote it) to try to figure out who the aspiring rocker is. After the writer is identified, he or she can give a brief back story behind that tidbit of personal information. This game brings out all kinds of interesting information. When I played this game with a group of friends, the rocker in the group turned out to be a mild-mannered accountant with short brown hair who has never been mistaken for Madonna.

These games give guests who don't know one another well an easy way to start one-on-one conversations later on. They can express an interest and ask the person about how she got interested in her hobby, or ask about some other personal information she had mentioned. Getting-to-know-you games are great icebreakers. When you can't think of anything particularly brilliant to say, you can still come across as a great conversationalist by talking to someone about his or her interests, and that's no lie!

My Favorite Things Party

I sometimes read articles on entertaining just for laughs. I am amused by glossy pictures of attractive, well-dressed guests standing around admiring the elaborate table decor while munching on appetizers that took longer to make than the party will actually last. I often imagine the hostess of this entertaining fantasy is not in the picture because she has passed out on the couch from exhaustion.

Why not have a party where the overworked hostess is not forced to use psychic abilities to predict what her guests would enjoy in food and entertainment? Let your guests feed and entertain themselves by having a My Favorite Things Party. On the invitation make it clear that each guest is responsible for bringing three things: a favorite food, a favorite object, and a few brochures from a favorite destination.

Where the invitation requests bringing a favorite food, be clear as to whether you are requesting appetizers or desserts, and mention how many people are expected at the party. If the dishes people offer to bring tend to be convenience-store cuisine, like Twinkies and Coke, it will be up to you as the hostess to balance the menu. Include both sweet and salty dishes, some healthy dishes, and some downright decadent dishes complemented by a variety of drinks.

A favorite thing can be just about anything portable as long as it's not a pet. If you wanted Rover at your party you would have invited the little yapper. Some ideas for favorite things would be bringing a favorite book, wearing a favorite piece of clothing, or sharing a favorite game. Encourage guests to get into the game with small portable games that can be played in a reasonably short period of time and are easy to learn. A party is not the time to break out the chess set.

Music also counts as a favorite thing. On the party invitation encourage guests to e-mail you a brief list of their favorite party music. It's fairly cheap to download a selection of the tunes off the Internet. Include guest favorites in your music rotation only if they enhance the cheerful mood you are trying to create. Upbeat instrumental tunes suggested by guests go on the party play list, screaming heavy metal music, not so much.

Favorite places might include favorite restaurants, shopping destinations, or vacation spots. Guests who don't have a brochure handy can print information from the Web site for their favorite place. For a more intimate party, say fewer than twelve people, you can gather everyone in a circle for the My Favorite Things group discussion after everyone has had a chance to grab a bite to eat. Have guests take turns briefly talking about the favorite thing they brought and their favorite destination. After everyone has had a chance to share, serve another round of drinks, set up a game table for anyone interested in playing (set out your own games if no one else brought one) and put the destination brochures on another table.

Having guests bring things that give them pleasure directs the conversation toward pleasant topics, thereby preventing the party from shifting into group therapy mode when everyone starts talking about personal problems. People should enjoy this party because it's all about them and what makes them happy. The guests are doing most of the entertainment-related work, which allows the hostess to do one of her favorite things, have fun!

Will Work for Food Party

Sometimes it seems like a to-do list is just an endless collection of thankless tasks that just get replaced by more thankless tasks every time you finish one task. Instead of whining your way through a time-consuming task, why not turn it into a social occasion?

Pick a task--such as organizing the basement, planting vegetable seeds or painting a room--that can be done with simple instructions and without a lot of heavy labor. Plan an easy to fix meal and invite a small group of friends over for a Will Work for Food party. Explain the purpose of the party and how much time will be spent on the task on the invitation. For example, state on the invitation that organizing your closets will take place from 10 a.m. to noon, followed by a lunch of salads and sandwiches.

Pick a task that can be completed within a few hours, or plan on getting as much done within a predetermined time period and finishing up yourself after the party is over. Thank guests for their time and efforts. If you want to be a truly gracious host, volunteer your time when one of your guests decides to have her own Will Work for Food party.

The Figure-Friendly Ice Cream Social

Before everyone and his dog started dieting, it was safe to have an ice cream social. The host would buy a giant tub of vanilla ice cream and a variety of toppings, invite people over, and everyone would indulge in the sweet pleasure of eating ice cream on a hot day. The last ice cream social I attended, only about half of the (female) guests actually ate dessert. The other half politely declined any offer of ice cream and acted pleasant while secretly wishing the diet sodas they were sipping tasted a lot more like hot-fudge sundaes.

Instead of fighting the diet epidemic, why not go with the flow and host an ice cream social that everyone can enjoy? Explain on the invitation that this is a figure-friendly affair. Desserts that come in individual servings, like Skinny Cow ice cream sandwiches or Weight Watchers frozen desserts, are faster and easier to serve than scooping out individual servings from a carton. If it's just not an ice cream social to you without vanilla ice cream and toppings, try one of the low-fat low-calorie brands such as Edy's.

Put out fresh fruit, such as strawberries, for topping ice cream. You can make strawberry sauce by mashing the berries and adding a dash of sugar for sweetness. Or mash some peach slices and add a dash of ground ginger for flavor. It's indulgence without regret that allows dieters to enjoy themselves as much as everyone else. No more diet soda!

Now *That's* Italian! Summer Party

Celebrate *la dolce vita* (the good life) with a Now *That's* Italian! vacation party. With a little planning and creativity you can bring the spirit of Italy to your own backyard. Play music with an Italian theme throughout the party. The romantic, sweeping songs of Andre Bocelli and the enchanting Italian soundtrack from *A Room with a View* would set the mood beautifully.

Late afternoon or early evening when the heat of day is passing are great times to hold an outdoor party. The perfect lazy summer afternoon outdoor game is bocce ball, an Italian game like croquet, only without the mallets. Bocce ball requires a little effort, needs little strategy, and is a whole lot of fun. The game consists of throwing a ball to knock your opponents' balls around on the ground. Like any classic party game, it is easy to learn and understand and requires just enough basic skill to keep things interesting.

Whether you are serving a meal or just drinks and dessert, an Italian-theme party calls for great food. A fresh green salad; a few kinds of cold pasta salads; and an antipasto tray with olives, artichoke hearts, crackers, and cheeses, for example, are satisfying dishes. If you decide to go with just desserts and drinks, schedule the party in between meals and make it clear on the invitation that you are serving light refreshments and desserts only. A variety of Italian sodas and tiramisu (a layered dessert served cold) can generally be found at better grocery stores. Check local ice cream and coffee shops for gelato, a low-fat dessert that resembles ice cream. Italian ice (shaved ice that can easily be made with frozen fruit juice ice cubes using a blender) is another refreshing option.

Wine complements a whole meal or just desserts equally well. If the cost of buying enough wine for everyone looks like a passport to the poorhouse, encourage guests to bring a bottle of Italian wine and join in a toast to *la dolce vita,* remembering that the good life is wherever friends and family gather to celebrate.

Save Money on Food without Starving Your Guests

Enjoy Restaurant-Style Dining at Home

Dining out is such a relaxing experience. As I enjoy the great food and pleasant conversation with my dining companions, I start to think I should dine out more often. Then the bill comes, and I suddenly remember why I don't dine out more often. Between the tips and the no-frills drinks like soda that cost several times what they would at a supermarket, even a basic meal without a lot of extras really adds up.

Thanks to the Internet, you and your guests can enjoy restaurant-style dining without the restaurant prices. Popular recipes from well-known restaurants are available online for free. When I say popular restaurants I am not talking about the latest over-hyped, trendy eatery. I am talking restaurants like the carbohydrate lover's perennial favorite, Panera Bread, providing online recipes. If your favorite restaurant isn't generous enough to list recipes on its Web site, check out copycat recipes from sites such as All Restaurant Recipes (all-restaurantrecipes.com) for listings of popular recipes. Many of the featured recipes are easy enough to appeal to home cooks who love great food but lack five-star cooking talent.

Now that you have cleverly selected time-tested, crowd-pleasing recipes, it's time to start cooking for an appreciative crowd. Invite a handful of friends for a meal, or schedule a gathering between mealtimes and serve smaller, budget-friendly dishes such as appetizers or desserts. To set the mood, give your home-style restaurant a name like "The Copycat Café." On a portable chalkboard, list the menu items under "Today's Specials." Approach guests with the phrase, "Hello, my name is (pick a name) and I will be your hostess tonight." For added effect you can write down drink orders on a small pad of paper. A small, simple floral centerpiece, the kind that's found in nice restaurants, on top of an elegant tablecloth is really all you need, besides pleasant background music, to set the mood.

After the empty dishes are cleared and before dessert is served, pass around a "tip" jar with a pen and small slips of paper. Instruct each guest to write a short recipe or entertaining tip and put it in the jar. After everyone has added a tip, serve dessert. While everyone is enjoying dessert, take the tips out of the jar one by one to read out loud. Just for fun, see if guests can match the tip to the person who wrote it.

Time to Save Some Cash

An essential ingredient to saving money when entertaining is timing. Inviting people over to your place during the dinner hour and preparing an entire meal complete with appetizers and a meat course is much more expensive than an afternoon brunch with some sort of egg dish, like frittata, accompanied by a selection of muffins and fruit. Where a superb evening meal calls for a fine wine, an afternoon brunch calls for fruit juice and maybe iced tea or coffee. To put a more celebratory spin on your get-together, include mimosas--half a glass of orange juice topped off by half a glass of champagne--with your brunch. You can splurge a little on the champagne because the orange juice makes the champagne go farther.

An evening cocktail party that includes a variety of appetizers and high-quality alcohol can leave you with a hangover of debt. If you are in the mood for a few cocktails and lots of company, ask local bars or restaurants whether they have a separate room where you and your guests can party. When you invite guests make it clear that you are simply arranging a get-together for cocktails. You aren't treating everyone to appetizers and appletinis.

Inviting people for coffee and dessert is an affordable way to play hostess. Either treat it like a dessert exchange, having everyone bring one dessert to share, or offer a selection of cookies, muffins, pastries, or other desserts that do not require time-consuming slicing during the social. If you serve cake or pie, cut it into different-size slices (to satisfy different-size appetites) ahead of time. Even if you serve gourmet coffee, this type of social is still a pretty sweet deal.

Cheap Snacks for Casual Get-Togethers

Serving food at any type of social get-together in your home is an essential part of being a gracious host. But it doesn't have to be an expensive part. You can satisfy your guests' appetites inexpensively by combining cheap foods with slightly more expensive ones.

Dips are a great example of this. Buy a bag or two of blue corn chips, which are not only fairly cheap but one of the healthier chips out there. Now splurge a little on some tasty fresh salsa. Any respectable grocery store should have fresh salsa made in store that hasn't been sitting on the shelf for a month.

Bread is a wonderfully cheap and filling snack. A long loaf of French bread sliced into small pieces is a chic way to satisfy a hungry crowd. Slice the loaf down the middle lengthwise and then cut the loaf into 3/4-inch slices. For the gourmet touch you can buy specially flavored olive oils or specialty spreads for dipping. For a dipping sauce that's as cheap or even cheaper than a loaf of French bread, check out your grocery store's selection of oil-based salad dressings.

Take a step up from your standard Chex mix and make your own easy mix instead. Mix a can of premium quality mixed nuts and a bag of small stick pretzels in a bowl. How easy is that? Some guests may be allergic to nuts, so be sure to have some nut-free snacks on hand as well.

This high/low approach to hosting works when adding the cost of beverages to the mix. For example, you can offer different cheap desserts, like cookies from a can, brownies from a mix, or homemade baked apples, and then serve premium coffee to wash all those affordable goodies down. These are just a few of the delicious ways to save on entertaining. By keeping your eyes open to interesting possibilities when food shopping, you are sure to come up with even more great ideas.

Cool Ice Cubes Infuse Your Drinks with Flavor

Ice cubes generally come in two forms. There is the traditional ice cube that gradually turns any drink into flavored water when left in the drink too long. Then there are the plastic gel filled, reusable ice cubes that come in all kinds of fruit, flower, or other kitschy designs. In addition to taking up space in the glass, these tacky little plastic delights have to be hand washed. Yippee, more housework!

Instead of diluting your drinks with ice, why not use ice cubes to infuse the drink with more flavor? Fill your ice cube tray with lemonade and use the lemonade ice cubes instead of lemon slices in your iced tea. Add a flavorful twist to plain iced tea with frozen ice cubes made of fruit drinks, such as peach and orange juice.

Ice cubes can also enhance the flavor of the drink by mimicking flavors that were already there. Lemon lime ice cubes made from fruit juice can be added to a lemon lime soda to maintain the flavor of the drink. Lemon lime ice cubes would also add a subtle hint of lime to lemonade while not watering down the original lemon taste. If flavored ginger ale or flavored water is what you're after, any kind of fruit juice frozen into cubes should do the trick. Be creative in mixing and matching drink and ice cube flavors, and add some pizzazz and variety to your party drink menu.

A Cool Idea for a Cheap Dessert

The traditional recipe for granita involves mixing sugar, flavorings such as fresh fruit, and water, then freezing the mix and shaving off bits of ice for an effect similar to a frozen snow cone. Personally, I don't want to put in that much time and effort to produce a glorified ice cube. An easier approach would be simply freezing fruit juice in an ice cube tray, placing the frozen cubes in a food blender, and then scooping out the frozen treat and placing it in a nice bowl to serve to guests as a dessert.

To create a more interesting dessert, use a blended drink that combines different juices, like a mango-peach-banana juice. Look for interesting juice blends at your local supermarket next to the refrigerated orange juice.

Get Out of the House

Turn Window-Shopping into a Girlfriend Get-Together

A change of the seasons means fresh ideas for your home and wardrobe are hitting the stores. What better time to get together with a few fashionable friends at an upscale shopping area for lunch and a free lesson in style? As you and your gathering of gal pals enjoy a leisurely afternoon of window-shopping, note the current design trends. Keep an eye out for colors, shapes, and materials that seem to be featured prominently. Pay special attention to interesting tabletop and furniture arrangements in home decor merchandise, the creative way clothing and accessories are put together on a mannequin, or anything else that could be translated to everyday use. I call this retail to reality.

After satisfying your appetite for the latest trends, pop into a local bistro for lunch. During lunch compare notes with your gal pals on anything you saw on display that could be imitated in your own dress or home decor without spending a fortune. Shopping for inspiration is a cheap and easy way to connect with your friends while learning about current trends and developing your own sense of style.

Local Attractions Offer Cheap Entertainment

Summertime and the entertaining is easy … if you take a more relaxed approach to entertaining. Summer entertaining can be as simple as arranging a get-together at your local farmers' market. Some farmers' markets sell crafts, host cooking demonstrations, and provide live music. It's a good idea to research your local farmers' markets by checking out Web sites to see what they offer, discover what time the live entertainment starts, and verify their hours of operation. When you call your friends or send out invitations to meet, be sure to include helpful information with the invitation such as directions and an easily identifiable landmark, like a clock tower, where you can rendezvous. To find farmers' markets in your area go to localharvest.org.

Your local parks and recreation Web sites are full of summertime entertaining ideas. Concerts in the park are often cheap or free altogether. Invite your friends to meet at your house for food and drinks before the concert. Enjoying food and drinks before the concert prevents you from wasting money on the overpriced junk food sold at the park. Carpooling from the house to the concert ensures that everyone arrives together. Naturally, a social guru like you did her homework to find out what to bring to the concert. Is seating provided, or do you need to bring lawn chairs or a blanket? Are bug repellent and bottled water necessary? Grass stains and bug bites can quickly turn happy campers into grumpy spoilsports. A little preparation can go a long way toward ensuring everyone has a good time.

Family entertainment centers are a great place to look for ideas. Anything designed to keep a five-year-old with zero attention span happy should easily keep your more grown-up crowd occupied. Try getting in the swing of summer by organizing a miniature golf tournament. Divide into two teams. The losing team buys pizza and drinks for the winners. If hitting a brightly colored ball through a windmill doesn't appeal to you, try go-carts or laser tag. Choose something fun and silly, and let the kid in you come out and play.

Book Club Express

For many busy readers the only thing harder than finding time to attend a book club meeting is finding time to read the assigned 600-page literary opus before the meeting. It's time to put that ten-pound behemoth of a book club selection down and introduce some time-saving tactics into your book club.

Meet at coffee houses, tea shops, or anywhere that can provide a quiet atmosphere and offer some light snacks and refreshments. Have the "host" e-mail members at least a week in advance with the time and location. Be sure to start the meeting at least an hour and a half before the coffee shop closes so you have plenty of time to sip and chat.

Short stories exist in just about every genre of book. Find an anthology, a collection of short stories, in the genre your club enjoys reading, and read one short story a month. Members should be able to read the story in one sitting. Because each book contains a collection of stories, members save money by buying fewer books.

A book club doesn't have to be limited to fiction. Nonfiction books, such as books on finance, can be broken down by reading a few chapters at a time. Each book club meeting could discuss those specific chapters instead of covering the whole book at once.

For the book club members who have a hard time sitting still long enough to read much of anything, audio books are worth looking into. Members can enjoy hearing dramatic narrative from their favorite books come to life while completing unexciting tasks like housework. Time-saving tactics like these make it easier for book club members to keep up and allow them to focus on the pleasures of reading or listening to a good book.

Shall We Dance?

Looking for a cheap way to enjoy some music, some socializing, and a whole lot of dancing? Take a class at a local dance studio. Classes that teach student dances like the tango or waltz may be more suitable for couples, but many classes are geared toward teaching an entire group without any pairing up. If the thought of waltzing into a dance class alone isn't appealing and you don't have a willing partner handy, grab a couple of gal pals and turn the dance class into a girls night out.

Before you hit the dance floor, check out your options online. The dance studio's Web site may give you insight as far as what to expect. It's helpful to know whether the class is for couples or more of a group class, and whether the class is for beginner or intermediate level dancers. Can you pay for one class at a time, or do you have to sign up for several classes? What is appropriate attire? Are special shoes required? Of course you know to wear comfortable clothes in breathable fabrics that allow for plenty of movement. But for most of the people in the class does that translate into jeans and a T-shirt, or simple flowing dresses that make the wearer look like she is ready to dance the night away at some fabulous party?

After an hour or two of waltzing, shimmying, swinging, and getting your groove on, the class is finished, but that doesn't mean the evening is over. Popular dance studios usually have a social hour after their evening classes. If they don't, you can create your own by inviting a few of your favorite dancing devotees to your place for some light snacks and refreshing drinks after the class.

Volunteering is Fabulous

In any decent-size metropolitan area in the U.S. you will find plenty of high-style social events and attractions. Typically some of the most fabulous local events, the ones that involve a dazzling fashion show, a delectable dining experience, and decor to die for, are also some of the most expensive to attend. The good news is that many of these events are for a charity. By volunteering for certain charities you can attend fancy fundraisers without going for broke buying tickets.

Many charities host fancy dinners and events as part of their fundraising efforts. Stuffing envelopes and calling for donations are great ways to support a charity, but they might not get you in the door of some of the more elegant events. If you want to participate in these upscale events, make sure part of your volunteer responsibilities require you to be physically present at the event. Volunteering for positions such as guest greeter or ticket taker allow you to experience the event up close and personal.

I am not suggesting attendance at fabulous events should be your only motivation for supporting a charity. What I am saying is that by giving of your time and efforts to a worthwhile charity and enjoying the occasional social outing for free as a result, you are creating a win-win situation for everyone.

Volunteering doesn't have to be limited to charitable events. Volunteering to be an usher at a local live theater lets you experience a variety of wonderful performances without having to buy a season ticket. No matter where you donate your time and efforts, volunteering can be your ticket to a truly enriching social life.

Of course volunteering can be a fun social outlet even without the fancy fundraisers. When you volunteer you usually find yourself surrounded by positive people who want to be there. This creates the type of environment that encourages camaraderie and friendships. Some forms of volunteering are good for your waistline as well as your social life. Instead of getting together at some restaurant to chat and chew, why not gather a group of friends and family to participate in a public charity walk, clean up a park, or plant trees? To see what volunteer opportunities are available in your area, check out volunteermatch.org.

Celebrating Holidays and Special Occasions

My Funny Valentine

Valentine's Day might not be the most obvious choice for a girlfriend get-together, but why not host a My Funny Valentine movie night for a handful of gal pals who enjoy romantic comedies? Send each guest a silly Valentine card as an invitation.

Feel free to ask guests to bring some sort of indulgent Valentine's Day theme food. Anything chocolate works, including chocolate dipped strawberries. For variety, offer different types of cut-up fruit as a snack option with chocolate fondue available for dipping. Accompany all those indulgent goodies with champagne and nonalcoholic bubbly drinks like sparkling water or Italian soda.

To make your budget-friendly get-together even more thrifty, schedule the My Funny Valentine movie night the first weekend after Valentine's Day. You and your guests will be able to buy Valentine's candy at deeply discounted prices. Keep the comedy coming after the movie is over by encouraging guests to talk about their funniest dating disasters or their favorite scenes from romantic movies.

Make Halloween a Movie Night

Halloween should be just as much fun for adults as it is for kids, so why not enjoy some grown-up entertainment by hosting something simple like a movie night? Pick a Halloween theme movie, preferably something PG that is fun and light in tone. I once attended a Halloween party where the main entertainment was a graphic slasher flick that killed my enthusiasm for the party almost as fast as the bad guy was killing off second-rate actors. A party is supposed to make guests loosen up, not lose their appetite.

It's pretty easy to build a general Halloween theme around a movie like *Ghostbusters*. Since the movie revolves around ghosts, you can ask guests on the invitation to come as the ghost of their favorite dead person. The dead person could be someone famous, a fictional character, or an eccentric deceased relative. Some people don't like dressing up in costumes for Halloween. To make everyone feel welcome with or without a costume, encourage guests to dress like mourners at a funeral and simply wear a lot of black--or all white for a ghostly effect.

Set the stage in a matter of minutes by throwing solid white sheets over the couch and chairs in the entertaining area. Turn the lights down a little if you have dimmers. If you happen to have a solid red tablecloth, maybe one left over from Christmas, use it to decorate whatever you are using as a buffet table.

For snacks set up a popcorn buffet. Mix a large batch of plain or lightly salted popcorn with a sweet candy like M&Ms in one large bowl. Mix another large batch of plain popcorn with Chex mix or trail mix for a saltier take on popcorn, and then mix up a third batch of popcorn and another type of candy, maybe gummy worms. Popcorn is so cheap that when you mix candy and popcorn equally, it ends up being much less expensive than serving candy by itself. For drinks you can serve soda pop and regular tea. Avoid overly flavorful teas that would clash with the taste of the popcorn.

If you are concerned about the party dying when the movie isn't on, buy a few Halloween theme games, like Halloween bingo, at your local toy store to bring your party back from the dead.

Creative Ways of Giving Thanks

Before December, when the Christmas season escalates into a credit card induced shopping frenzy, there is that little holiday called Thanksgiving. At Thanksgiving we take time to reflect on what we are grateful for, instead of all the stuff we hope to get. One popular tradition is to have everyone seated at the Thanksgiving table talk briefly about what they are thankful for. This attitude of gratitude usually disappears right after the last person utters the last words of gratitude and everyone starts thinking about how grateful they are that no one has scarfed down the last of the coveted mashed potatoes.

For small, intimate gatherings where adding a gift for each guest won't break the bank, consider giving pocket-size gratitude journals as a party favor. It's one party favor that keeps the spirit of the celebration alive long after Thanksgiving is over. Encourage guests to briefly note the things they are grateful for in the blank journal regularly, especially when they are stressed or bored.

Another way to expand on the theme of thanks is to encourage guests to bring a nonperishable food item to the Thanksgiving gathering to be donated to a local food pantry, or fun treats like packaged cookies for a local women's shelter.

For the hostess who looks at preparing an elaborate feast as more manual labor than a labor of love, go with an "I'm thankful I'm not doing dishes" Thanksgiving theme. Gather guests at a nice restaurant and enjoy one another's company and a tasty meal that allows everyone to relax, knowing that the pile of dirty dishes they are producing will be taken care of by someone else. After the meal take advantage of all that time saved by not cooking and cleaning by playing games, watching a movie, or just sharing in pleasant conversation.

Don't Be a Holiday Martyr

For anyone who is tired of the expense and labor involved in hosting large holiday gatherings, it's time to stop whining and start delegating! Delegating others into helping requires tact, flattery, and more sugar coating than a Christmas cookie. Give guests with any cooking talent at all a family recipe and tell them you know they'll do it justice, or simply ask them to bring a side dish while gushing enthusiastically about how you just know they'll come up with something great. For the guests with no cooking talent at all, suggest they buy a pie or two. Either way, be gracious in telling them you appreciate their help.

One easy way to get help with holiday decorating is to have a tree-trimming party. Serve nonalcoholic beverages for the first hour or so. Drinking and holiday decorating don't mix. Bring out enough decorations to keep your guests busy for at least an hour. Give your guests a few simple decorating tasks to choose from. Then give them supplies and a few helpful suggestions to get them started. Allowing guests to choose a decorating task makes them feel more like a participant than a servant. Set aside the more fragile decorations to handle yourself. After an hour or an hour and a half, check progress, set out some snacks and more drinks, and be sure to admire and compliment your guests on their handiwork.

Make it sound as though you are doing your guests a favor by volunteering to co-host a progressive dinner instead of hosting the entire meal yourself. Put a positive spin on it by mentioning how busy everyone is at this time of year and how a progressive dinner would allow guests to spend one, two, or all three courses of a meal together, whatever their schedule allows. Set specific times for each course, allowing about an hour for each. Volunteer for the appetizer, main course, or dessert course, making it clear that you expect other people to volunteer for the two other courses. Once you have mastered the art of delegating you can sit back and enjoy the holidays for a change.

Holiday Entertaining is in the Bag

Underneath all the pretty ribbon and gaudy wrapping paper, holiday wrap parties are a lot of work disguised as a party. Traditional wrap parties involved guests hauling their gifts (to people not invited to the wrap party) to the house of a host, wrapping a bunch of gifts, and then hauling the gifts they wrapped back to the their own homes. Guests should not be forced to haul a bunch of packages back and forth. That's what the UPS guy is for.

Lighten the load for your guest with a modern twist on the traditional wrap party. Attach a completed invitation to an empty paper gift bag with a caption like "A good time is in the bag" or "You are invited to my holiday bag lady party," and mail it at least two weeks before the party. On the invitation explain that the purpose of the party is to decorate gift bags that your guests can later use for holiday gifts. Guest can bring old holiday cards with nothing written on the back side of the picture, glue stick, stamps, paints, wrapping paper remnants, or other small objects that could be attached to a gift bag.

As the host you will be supplying plain bags and glue sticks if no one else is bringing those items. An assortment of bargain bags can be bought in bulk through Oriental Trading (orientaltrading.com) or your local dollar store. Glossy bags may not absorb decorative paint very well, so avoid those if you intend to paint the bags.

Now you are ready to party. Set up an area, preferably a large table, with scissors and supplies. One thing you won't have to worry about as a host is finding the perfect party favor. At this party the guests are actually creating their own party favors. Impress your guests and anticipate their gift-giving needs by having at least three different-size bags for each guest.

Have a few snacks, both the healthy and indulgent kind, and some hot drinks like cider or cocoa near the party table. Put on some holiday music. For added entertainment, turn listening to instrumental holiday music into a game by having guests name that tune or try to sing as many lyrics as they can remember while they create their one-of-a-kind gift bags.

Holiday Lights Tour

With a little planning, a leisurely drive through parks or neighborhoods featuring holiday lights displays can become a friendly get-together on wheels. Check local newspapers, tourist Web sites, and parks and recreation Web sites for locations of holiday lights displays. After choosing a display, invite a handful of people to participate in your holiday lights tour. If the number is small enough, you may be able to fit into one vehicle. If the number is larger than six or no one in your party owns a minivan, take two cars and keep in contact with stragglers via cell phone.

Have guests meet at your home. Don't serve drinks before the tour. Drinking a lot of liquids before taking a long drive creates a potentially uncomfortable situation for passengers. Homeowners with display lights expect people to admire their handiwork from afar. Their holiday spirit might not extend to letting a bunch of strangers use their bathroom.

Before starting out on your journey you need a detailed map and a co-pilot in the front passenger seat who can read a map. As soon as your guests are settled into the vehicle, start playing holiday music to set the mood. Soft instrumental music is more conducive to conversation. Subjecting your passengers to annoyingly perky songs about Frosty the Snowman will probably receive a rather frosty response.

It helps to have someone acting as a host if it will be a long drive to your destination. The host can quiz passengers on such topics as what are the twelve things listed in the song "The Twelve Days of Christmas" or have guests talk about their favorite holiday memories. A host with an irreverent sense of humor can also act as a tour conductor, keeping a running commentary on the displays "… and folks, if you look to your left you will see the world's tackiest collection of plastic Santas…" After the tour is finished, head back to your house for hot drinks and a few snacks and reminisce about your favorite displays.

Flights of Fancy: How to Be Well Traveled

Feel Free to Act Like a Tourist

When I had an out-of-town guest to entertain for a weekend, we found plenty of ways to have fun for free. Our first stop was the Hallmark Visitors Center in Kansas City, a free museum dedicated to the history of Hallmark. Unlike other museums, which can be a bit stuffy, in this one we read musical cards that featured such fun ditties as "It's Raining Men," were shown how cards were made by a friendly printer who gave us golden cardboard crowns to wear, and watched sappy Hallmark commercials on TV monitors.

We followed up the Hallmark visit with an outing to a free outdoor antiques and crafts show. We looked at all the interesting things on display without buying any of them, just taking pleasure in being outdoors on such a beautiful day. After all that walking, we went to lunch to refuel and do some people-watching at a restaurant with outdoor seating on the Plaza (an outdoor shopping area). It was like a free fashion show with a mix of high style, low style, and people with no style. Lunch was followed by window-shopping wonderful fashion and home decor displays. Having refueled and with plenty of the day left, we went to the Nelson Atkins Museum of Art, which happened to be free to the public that Saturday. After enjoying the artwork inside, we walked around the sculpture garden outside the museum.

We still had plenty of time before the sun went down, so we visited a local park and walked around for a while. After burning calories all day, we decided to eat at a local safari theme restaurant and enjoyed a perfect ending to a great day.

My more-mature companion paid for the meal, partly as a thank-you for my acting as chauffeur and partly to take advantage of the senior citizens discount the restaurant offered. The point of this long-winded story is that if you are willing to be resourceful and do some walking, you can act like a typical tourist without spending like one!

Factory Tours Offer Frugal Fun

When I think of fun and exciting things to do, taking a tour of a factory that cranks out widgets is not the first thing that comes to mind. However, a brief tour of a Web site called factorytoursusa.com had me thinking a factory tour just might be the perfect entertainment to occupy visiting relatives for the holidays or for staycations (vacations you take within your home state as a cheap alternative to a long-distance vacation). Factory tours are generally very cheap or free.

Factorytoursusa.com conveniently lists factory tours by state. Among the listings for factories that produce things like recreational vehicles, I found factory tours for a candy factory and a muffin factory in my state. I would definitely consider deepening my understanding of factory operations if the factory in question happens to give out free sweets with every tour.

Do Your Homework Before Hitting the Road

Before the summer is over, consider adding a trip to a quaint small town where you can enjoy yourself at a leisurely pace in the warm sunshine. To make the most of your trip, do some research first. Beware of travel brochures and Web sites for small towns that use words like "quaint" and "charming" but don't go into detail about what attractions the town has to offer.

One summer some friends of mine visited a local small town known for its wineries and its well-attended, alcohol-fueled Oktoberfest. I asked them what their visit was like. They said it was OK, but it would probably be more fun to visit during the Oktoberfest. Apparently the less sober you are the more appealing the town is.

If there is a specific attraction you want to see, call ahead to be sure it is open when you want to see it. During one family visit, I knew there was a piece of art at a local museum that was a particular family favorite. We drove to the museum, only to find that the piece of art was in storage and not available for viewing. This letdown was followed by a visit to a local small town, only to discover that the ice cream parlor listed in its tourist brochure was closed. We didn't visit that town just for the ice cream, but it had been one of the things we were looking forward to. After two disappointments, I got smart and called the restaurant we were considering eating dinner at. The restaurant didn't answer the phone so we made other plans. I later found out it was just open for lunch.

Supplies for any road trip include ice water and nutrition bars to stave off hunger pangs and grumpy passengers. A car window can act as a tanning booth, so apply sunscreen before entering the car. It's always a good idea to carry cash in the form of small bills; not every small-town vendor can make change for a hundred-dollar bill or accept credit cards.

Always have a printed map with you when going to an area you are not familiar with. Don't rely solely on fancy electronic GPS gadgets. A friend and I were taking a designer home tour in a part of town we weren't familiar with. My friend, who was driving, wanted to show off her new GPS device. The device directed us to a house that was fully occupied and definitely not part of the homes tour. In spite of being given the correct address, the tracking device was off by several blocks. Luckily I had gone to mapquest.com and printed out a map with the correct location. If my experiences have taught me anything, it's that spontaneity is overrated. Better to do some research and be prepared. Happy trails!

Thrifty Travel Tips

The desire to see new places and have experiences you simply can't get at home is so strong that it's easy to get swept up in the adventure of travel and lose sight of the real costs involved. You get so focused on the big expenses, like plane tickets and hotels, that you overlook the small expenses … that is, until the credit card bill comes.

On one vacation my travel companions and I decided to pay a little more for a rental car with a GPS navigational system, thinking it would be more accurate than a map. When we tried to locate our destination from our hotel address on King Street, the GPS system brought up several local King Streets preceded by north, southeast or west, as in East King Street. The problem was that our hotel was simply on King Street, just King Street. After trying other features on the GPS system to get some sort of useful directions, we gave up and reverted back to the printed paper map.

Food is a big expense while traveling. If a free breakfast is included with your hotel stay and it consists of something more appetizing than a stale donut and lukewarm coffee, then by all means take advantage of it. For lunch and dinner you will probably have your choice of everything from sandwich shops to nicer restaurants. Frequent the nicer restaurants during lunchtime when the menu is generally cheaper, and save the bargain sandwich shops for dinner meals.

Some tourist-friendly travel destinations provide local buses, trolleys, or even boats for getting around. To save cash on transportation, cluster your activities around the same area. If you are interested in one attraction across town, look into other attractions and restaurants in the same area so you can hit them all at once and not have to pay for multiple rides in opposite directions.

All that sightseeing can work up an appetite, but expect anything that comes out of a hotel vending machine to be ridiculously overpriced. Ask the hotel desk clerk for the location of the nearest drug store or supermarket, and stock up on soda pop and snacks there. If you want to be a truly thrifty traveler, bring your own energy snack bars, such as Luna Bars, and carry an empty water bottle with you that you can fill whenever you come across a drinking fountain.

Skip the tacky souvenir T-shirts and shot glasses, and instead of buying postcards take lots of digital photos to remember your trip by. Plan ahead, and the one souvenir you won't be returning home with is a fat credit card bill.

Girlfriend Getaways

If you want to take a vacation that's all about you, try a girlfriend getaway. Unlike family vacations where frazzled moms are expected to do the planning and keep everyone happy throughout the entire vacation, girlfriend getaways are actually relaxing! As much as I am sure you love your family, if you really want to relax on vacation my advice is that you should take a vacation *from* your family, not *with* them.

Picking compatible gal pals is just as important as picking a destination. You want someone who enjoys the same kind of activities and is willing to work within the budget you have in mind (a five-star hotel isn't cheap even if you share a room and split the cost). Another important point is attitude. For some women, lying around doing little or nothing represents the ultimate in relaxation and bliss. Other women adopt the attitude of "I didn't travel all this way to do nothing." For these women, making the most of a vacation means seeing and doing new things. Have a long chat with potential travel mates about their idea of an ideal vacation before proposing any kind of trip together.

Girlfriend getaways have become so popular in recent years that entire Web sites are now devoted to them. One site that understands traveling women and their needs is Girlfriend Getaways (girlgetaways.com). This site includes such female-friendly articles as beauty and style, spas, and pampering. There are plenty of articles about travel that do not require a passport. For even more online travel inspiration, check out holidaygolightly.com. There, travel categories are conveniently broken down by interest or type of travel desired. Categories like active, food and wine, local culture tour, and shopping make it easy to quickly identify where to start your search for destinations. Some of the categories, like nightlife, are clearly geared towards party girls. Whether your idea of a vacation involves being pampered at a spa all day or partying all night, a girlfriend getaway represents an escape from the ordinary.

Final Thoughts

I hope the ideas in this book inspire you to be even more resourceful in creating your own opportunities to live well for less. Dare to be fabulous!

Resources

Books

Saving Money

The Green Year: 365 Small Things You Can Do to Make a Big Difference, by Jodi Helmer

Beauty

Looking Younger: Makeovers That Make You Look as Young as You Feel, by Robert Jones

The 5-Minute Face, by Carmindy

The Original Beauty Bible, by Paula Begoun

Fashion

How Not to Look Fat, by Danica Lo

Fashion for Dummies, by Jill Martin and Pierre A. Lehu

Home Decor

Slob Proof!, by Debbie Wiener

The House Always Wins, by Marni Jameson

Web Sites

Money

Catalogchoice.org

Craigslist.com

Directsalescareers.com

Dmachoice.org

Optoutprescreen.com

Stretcher.com

Thecheapdiva.com

Beauty

Beautypedia.com

Beautyschoolsdirectory.com

Drugstore.com

Luckyscent.com

Massageregister.com

Scentiments.com

Totalbeauty.com

ULTA.com

Shopping

Amazon.com

Bathandbodyworks.com

Evesaddiction.com

eBay.com

Etsy.com

Orientaltrading.com

Shopittome.com

Target.com

Home Decor

Bedbathandbeyond.com

Bhg.com

Crateandbarrel.com

Marthastewart.com

Zgallerie.com

Leisure and Entertaining

All-restaurantrecipes.com

Apple.com

Factorytoursusa.com

Girlgetaways.com

Hallmarkvisitorscenter.com

Holidaygolightly.com

Localharvest.org

Mapquest.com

Meetup.com

Nelson-atkins.org

Panerabread.com

Spafinder.com

Volunteermatch.org

CPSIA information can be obtained at www.ICGtesting.com
Printed in the USA
LVOW071621231112

308559LV00016B/997/P

9 780982 529607